Distant Voices

Distant Voices

Discovering a Forgotten Past for a Changing Church

C. Leonard Allen

A·C·U
PRESS

Several paragraphs in this book are excerpted and adapted from the author's essay, "The Stone that the Builders Rejected: Barton W. Stone in the Memory of Churches of Christ," in *Cane Ridge in Context*, ed. Anthony Dunnavant (Nashville: Disciples of Christ Historical Society, 1992). Used by permission.

Copyright 1993
ACU Press, Abilene Christian University Press

Cover design, Trace Hallowell
Cover illustration, David Moses
Typesetting, Grant Graphics and Type

Printed in the United States of America

ISBN - paperback - 089112-154-4
ISBN - hardback - 0-89112-115-2
Library of Congress Card Number - 92-73842
First Edition

What was memory is dust
now, and many a story
told in shade or by the fire
is gone with the old light.
On the courthouse shelves
the facts lie mute
upon their pages...
lost in the silence of
old days and voices. And yet
the land and the mind
bear the marks of a history
that they do not record.

Wendell Berry
"Where" (1977)

Modernity began with an assault on tradition;
"Let us start over," said Descartes and Locke.
Slowly and with great reluctance we in the
modern world have come to realize that there
can be no starting over, no escape from heritage.

Nicholas Wolterstorff
"Remember to Remember" (1989)

To my mother,

Carolyn O. Allen,

with gratitude and love

Contents

List of Illustrations

Acknowledgements

A little over a year ago the worship committee at my home congregation, the Minter Lane Church of Christ in Abilene, Texas, asked me to prepare a series of historical vignettes centered around the theme of "heritage." The comments sparked by that short Sunday morning series encouraged me to expand the material. This book is the result.

With pleasure I acknowledge several people who assisted in this work.

I am indebted especially to R. L. Roberts for the numerous discussions over recent years which have greatly enriched my understanding and pointed me into fruitful avenues of research; to Doug Foster for his interest in and encouragement of this work through its final stages; and to Richard Hughes for the friendship over many years and the stimulus of continuing conversation.

Stan Reid, Steve Weathers, Fran Winkles, Norman Parks, Marge Wood, Don and Latimer Bowen, and Pat Brooks also deserve a special word of thanks for their assistance and encouragement. My graduate assistant Terry Seufferlein diligently tracked down a host of materials and helped in other vital ways, and to him I owe a considerable debt.

Dean Ian Fair of the College of Biblical Studies at ACU has encouraged and enabled my work in significant ways. I have been blessed to work under his leadership.

Roberta Brown, faculty assistant in the College of Biblical Studies, again provided wonderful support. Week by week she maintained a steady enthusiasm for this project that helped keep me going amid the heavy press of other duties.

And finally, to my wife, Holly, I owe another special thanks.

C. Leonard Allen
July 1992

Chapter 1

Discovering a Forgotten Past

It's what we forget that defines us,
and stays in the same place,
And waits to be rediscovered.

—Charles Wright (1981)

<hr>

When I think back to my elementary school experience only a few events from those six rich and formative years remain sharp and vivid in my memory. There was the day my second grade teacher slapped me on the face for no apparent reason, and the day in the fourth grade when I was chosen next to last for kickball teams. There was the week we made papiermaché globes, and that glorious day when our class took a field trip to hear a symphony orchestra for the first time. And there was the day in the fifth grade when I was elected lieutenant of the school safety patrol.

Many days and events in those six years of school were as important as these, I'm sure, but for reasons I do not understand these events were burned into my memory. To this day they comprise key episodes in the "history" of my early schooling. A good bit of the rest remains dim and fuzzy.

Our memories work like that. Certain experiences become decisive ones for the story of our lives, while most others—for reasons which largely escape us—take up minor places in the story or simply fade into the nether regions of memory.

Our lives are full of a vast array of experiences both great and small. Those experiences pile up quickly and, as it were, lie about in a vast, unmanageable heap. We attempt to make sense of them, to order and interpret them. By some hidden workings of the mind, certain events get imprinted indelibly in our memories while others get blotted out or remembered only with some difficulty.

Our pasts are like an expanse of dark water lit up from within by a few bright lights. Peering down into it, we see some things clearly, while many others appear shadowy and distorted. And some things we see not at all. As poet Charles Wright put it recently,

> Places swim up and sink back, and days do,
> The edges around what really happened
>   we'll never remember
> No matter how hard we stare back at the past.

The fact is that our memories are highly selective. In order to make sense of things, we simplify intricate and tangled events, making plausible—and sometimes implausible—connections between them. We assign motives to people and dress up our own. And we simply drop out parts of the story that are too painful or that don't seem to fit in the overall story.

We might even say that, in one sense, we create our pasts. Out of the daily flood of experiences, we fashion a coherent story of our lives. The particular past that we remember thereby takes on a certain pattern and tenor.

That remembered past powerfully influences our

present lives. It does much to determine how we think of ourselves and how we relate to others. It limits and focuses the goals we set, the challenges we will accept, the dreams we are willing to dream. It helps us determine what we can and cannot become.

But sometimes things happen that change the past we remember. Sometimes a long-forgotten or unknown event, when recalled or learned, recasts parts of the story, helping us see the whole story in a new light. "So that's what really happened!" we exclaim. "My father didn't really mean all those things in the way that I remembered them," we discover. "There was a whole different side to the story that I never saw before," we come to understand.

When that happens we may find ourselves slowly fashioning a new past, one made up of new memories, new insights, and new angles on old memories. That expanded and revised story may be one with somewhat less resplendent heroes and somewhat tamer villains. Or, for some people, it may be a story with episodes of unimagined hurt that they could not bear to remember and yet could never get over by forgetting.

Seeing the past in a new light, however, can bring clarifying perspective and healing balm. It can help one clear up imagined hurts and bring healing to unimagined, terribly real ones. It can provide the impetus toward reconciling old estrangements. It can make the future look different.

The way we "remember" our Christian past or tradition parallels somewhat the way we remember our own personal pasts. Our "memories" of our Christian heritage are also selective. As the story of a religious movement is passed on, some things get dropped out and forgotten; intricate events get simplified; conflicts get enshrined and differences exaggerated; lines of separation get hardened. Furthermore, as with our individual memories, discovering lost or forgotten parts of this past can bring clarifying perspective—and perhaps healing balm—to Christian life today.

This book is an exercise in remembering. It has one overarching purpose: to recover some of the forgotten or "distant voices" from the modern history of Churches of Christ.

I use the phrase "distant voices" in a double sense: first, "distant" simply in that these voices come from a time now long past; but second, and more importantly, "distant" in that they are the minority voices among Churches of Christ, the voices that have been drowned out, the softer, fainter voices. Some of the voices come from people largely forgotten by the tradition; others come from major, well-known figures who held certain views now largely forgotten.

We easily assume that the history of Churches of Christ is basically "the present writ small." One may assume, in other words, that Alexander Campbell and his colleagues restored New Testament faith and order sometime in the early nineteenth century and that Churches of Christ—or at least some segment of them—have simply preserved that pattern of truth unchanged down to the present time. Today one may see a fairly fixed, uniform tradition and easily assume that this has been the story from near the movement's beginnings.

But it was not. As the tradition formed through the nineteenth and down to the early twentieth century, certain voices assumed central, controlling positions, thereby pushing other voices to the margins. These more dominant voices shaped the tradition of twentieth-century Churches of Christ. They set the boundaries of acceptable views. They defined orthodoxy. They also interpreted, shaped, and maintained the "memory" or story of the movement, and this shaped story made clear who stood at the center and who at the margins.

But these central, more powerful voices were not, simply by virtue of their power, necessarily the wisest or most astute. As Walter Brueggemann has put it, "the capacity to give authoritative interpretation [within a tradition] is a matter of social power, and not primarily a matter of insight or sensitivity." Important insights may reside at the margins of a tradition as well as at its center, among the minority as well as the majority.

Churches of Christ are now in a time when the central or dominant voices of the twentieth-century tradition are being questioned—gently by some, more sharply by others. It is a time when many people are assessing their spiritual heritage, indeed, a time when the traditional settlement of center and margin is coming under critical review.

In such a time, it helps to hear some of the "distant voices," those who once occupied a strong place in the tradition but whose views have been remembered selectively, screened out, or simply forgotten. Listening to such voices helps one glimpse a modern heritage that is broader, richer, and more diverse than one presently may suppose.

Out of such listening can arise a new and perhaps more faithful settlement of center and margin.

Selected Sources

Epigraph: Charles Wright, *The Southern Cross* (New York: Random House, 1981), p. 65.

Brueggemann, Walter. *Interpretation and Obedience: From Faithful Reading to Faithful Living*. Minneapolis: Fortress, 1991.

Chapter 2

Communion Festivals in Kentucky

The spirit of partyism, and party distinctions, were apparently forgotten.... The spirit of love, peace, and union, were revived.... Happy days! joyful seasons of refreshment from the presence of the Lord.

—Barton Stone (1827)

W hen Barton Warren Stone accepted a call from two small Presbyterian congregations in Bourbon County, Kentucky, in the fall of 1798, he had no idea that he soon would play a central role in the greatest revival in American history.

Stone at that time was a young, unmarried Presbyterian preacher. He had been converted in 1791 during a revival in North Carolina sparked by the preaching of the fiery Presbyterian James McGready. He had applied to the Orange Presbytery for a ministerial license and completed the necessary seminary training. In 1796 he had passed the examination and received his preaching license.

After a period of itinerant preaching, Stone moved into central Kentucky in 1798 to begin a long ministry with the two small, somewhat troubled congregations at Cane Ridge and Concord.

In May of 1801 Stone traveled southwest from Cane Ridge to Logan County, near the Tennessee line, to visit his old friend James McGready. In the previous three years revivals had broken out in McGready's congregations at Red River, Muddy River, and Gasper River. The revivals had become famous and Stone wanted to see what all the excitement was about. Many hundreds gathered on this occasion, and Stone witnessed dozens of people struck down in a swoon-like state.

When Stone returned to Cane Ridge and Concord and told the story of what he had witnessed, revival immediately broke out there. People began to come under deep conviction. Some fell down or swooned, just as he had witnessed at Gasper River in southern Kentucky.

As the summer approached, the revival began to spread around central Kentucky. It would reach its climax at Cane Ridge in early August.

The gatherings at which these revivals occurred usually have been called camp meetings, but that term is somewhat misleading. They were actually communion festivals following a two-hundred-year-old tradition rooted deeply in Scotch-Irish Presbyterianism.

The communion festival originated in the Scottish churches of the early to mid 1600s. Seeking to imitate the New Testament observance, the church leaders served communion on long dinner tables set up in the aisles of the church buildings. They set the tables with white linen tablecloths and napkins, and people sat around them as if for a regular meal. Servers passed large platters of bread and flagons of wine, and people ate, not tiny token amounts, but the amount they might consume at an actual meal. At a large communion service as many as ten waves of communicants might fill the tables, and the communion meal might last all day.

By the mid 1600s this communion service had expanded into a three to five day event. It usually began on Friday or Saturday with long and intense preparation sermons. Ministers warned people about coming to the table unprepared, without pure hearts. They carefully screened candidates and gave admission tokens to those judged fit to commune. Following the all-day communion service on Sunday, a thanksgiving service on Monday ended the communion season.

The communion festivals became the highlight of the church year. People came from many miles around to attend. For serious believers they were times of intense self-examination and spiritual renewal; for young people they were times of conviction and conversion. Sometimes these communion festivals exploded with revival, including intense physical and emotional effects such as fainting and trance-like states.

The most famous of the Scottish communions occurred at Cambuslang, near Glasgow, in August 1742. It was an event strikingly similar to the one at Cane Ridge. According to estimates, attendance surpassed 30,000; at the all-day Sunday service 3,000 took communion. The famous evangelist George Whitefield preached the thanksgiving sermon on Monday. Many physical "exercises" were reported—falling, fainting, loud outcries, and others.

These revivalistic communion services aroused controversy and division in the Presbyterian Church of Scotland and Ireland. The Seceder branch of the church, to which Thomas and Alexander Campbell belonged, deeply opposed such trends, viewing them as disorderly and excessive.

As Scotch-Irish Presbyterians immigrated to America, they brought the communion festival with them. Indeed, it was precisely this kind of communion service that took place at Cane Ridge, Kentucky, on August 8, 1801.

The Cane Ridge communion was the climax of a dozen or so communion festivals in central Kentucky that summer. Colonel Robert Patterson, famed Indian fighter and one of the founders of Lexington, attended at least eight of those festivals and wrote descriptions in his journal.

One occurred in May at the congregation of Richard McNemar on Cabin Creek fifty miles from Cane Ridge. Fifty to sixty people fell or fainted. Another was held at the Concord congregation the last weekend in May. About 4,000 attended. Communion tables were set up outdoors under beech trees, and about 250 communed. At Stony Creek in early June 8,000 were present, and 250 fell or fainted. At Indian Creek a few weeks later 10,000 attended with 800 reportedly "slain."

Between May and November at least fifty Presbyterian congregations in Kentucky held four-day communion services, with about twelve of those linked closely to Cane Ridge.

The Cane Ridge communion began on Friday, August 6. About 140 wagons or carriages with perhaps 800 people camped on the grounds. A continual stream of people arrived throughout Saturday and Sunday. Attendance estimates ranged from 10,000 to over 20,000 (at a time when the population of nearby Lexington—Kentucky's largest town—was less than 1,800).

Perhaps as many as 2,500 were devout Presbyterians who came for the purpose of taking communion. The others were casual visitors or outsiders, most of whom, no doubt, held basic Christian beliefs. But they did not come for the communion service and probably did not even understand the Scottish communion tradition.

Saturday was the traditional day of preparation. But swelling crowds soon changed the central focus. A preaching

*The Cane Ridge meetinghouse where the communion service
was held during the 1801 revival.*

tent was erected on the grounds, and by Saturday afternoon
there was continual preaching from both the tent and the
meetinghouse. Excitement mounted. By sundown the cries
and shouts of the penitent could be heard throughout the
crowds. Indeed, the noise rose to a level that could be heard
several miles away.

The communion service took place in the meetinghouse on Sunday as scheduled. Robert Marshall preached
the traditional sermon outside and then the communicants
presented their tokens and entered the building. The tables
were set up in the aisles of the meetinghouse (probably in
the shape of a cross). Estimates of the number who partook
ranged from 700 to 1,100. They were seated around the tables
in shifts, perhaps 75 to 100 at a time. The communion service
was orderly, though it elicited deep emotion in many of the
communicants.

Outside the meetinghouse the scene was different: the groaning, cries, and falling continued. Some who fell remained conscious and talkative, but some fell into a deep coma-like state. Crowds gathered around the fallen. Some portions of the grassy ridge looked like a battlefield scattered with bodies. By Tuesday the estimate of the fallen rose to 3,000, though more likely estimates range between 500 and 1,000.

Observers had difficulty describing what they saw. One minister wrote:

> Sinners dropping down on every hand, shrieking, groaning, crying for mercy, convoluted; professors [of faith] praying, agonizing, fainting, falling down in distress, for sinners, or in raptures of joy! Some singing, some shouting, clapping their hands, hugging and even kissing, laughing; others talking to the distressed, to one another, or to opposers of the work, and all this at once—no spectacle can excite a stronger sensation.

People continued to arrive, and the revival continued until at least Wednesday, perhaps Thursday. Ministers had difficulty judging the number of conversions. Stone later estimated the number at between 500 and 1,000.

After Cane Ridge, the communion festivals in central Kentucky continued almost weekly until November. The revival fires also continued to burn. Conservative Presbyterian ministers reacted with deep apprehension. Their traditional faith included experiential conversion but they controlled it within strong institutional and doctrinal boundaries. At Cane Ridge, they feared, those boundaries were loosed or broken.

But some Presbyterian ministers rejoiced. Chief among them was Barton Stone. In 1827 he looked back on the events of 1801 with hearty approval. "The doctrine preached by all was simple, and nearly the same," he wrote. "All urged faith in the gospel, and obedience to it, as the way of life. The spirit of partyism, and party distinctions, were apparently forgotten....The spirit of love, peace, and union, were revived....Happy days! joyful seasons of refreshment from the presence of the Lord."

In the years that followed Cane Ridge, tensions over revivalism escalated. In late 1803 these tensions led Stone and five other pro-revival ministers to withdraw from the Synod of Kentucky and form the Springfield Presbytery. Nine months later, however, they disbanded. They issued a document entitled "The Last Will and Testament of the Springfield Presbytery" in which they renounced all names but "Christian" and all creeds but the Bible.

Under Stone's leadership the new "Christian" movement grew rapidly, so that by 1811 it could claim about 13,000 members. Detractors nicknamed them "New Lights," but Stone rejected the term, insisting that "we possess no new light; but only that old unsullied light which shines in the Bible."

The central themes of the movement were freedom from all creeds and coercive human traditions, restoration of simple primitive Christianity, the transforming power of the Holy Spirit, separation from the fashions of the world, and the millennial unity of believers.

Stone remained an ardent supporter of revival practices. Some of the physical "exercises" present in the 1801 revival—particularly the one Stone described as holy laughter or singing—apparently continued to be a part of the Cane Ridge and Concord churches for a decade or so under Stone's ministry.

Even with the admitted excesses, Stone could never condemn revivals like the one he helped lead at Cane Ridge. Writing many years after the great revivals, he said he had no doubt that they were "a good work—the work of God; nor has my mind wavered since on the subject." In the *Christian Messenger*, begun in 1826, Stone often inserted notices about people who "found a hope" at Methodist camp meetings; sometimes he would list the number of converts. "Shall we

Barton Stone's grave marker (foreground); behind it stands the stone sanctuary that now shelters and protects the Cane Ridge meetinghouse.

oppose a revival, because we think the conductors of it are ignorant of what we may deem the most important doctrine of the gospel?" he asked in 1831. "If genuine religion be the fruit of such revivals, we dare not reject it without incurring the divine displeasure."

The stirring events of the great Cane Ridge revival remained close to Stone's heart until the end of his life. In 1843, the year before his death, he returned to Cane Ridge for the last time. As he left the old meetinghouse, supported on one side by his son, he stopped suddenly and pointed to the ground with his cane. He said it was the site of the stand where he had preached during those memorable days of August 1801. He surveyed the scene, and his eyes filled with tears. Then he turned quickly to his carriage, and headed back home to Illinois.

Selected Sources

Epigraph: Stone, "History of the Christian Church," p. 77.

Conkin, Paul. *Cane Ridge: America's Pentecost*. Madison: University of Wisconsin, 1990.

Eslinger, Ellen T. "The Great Revival in Bourbon County, Kentucky." Ph.D. diss., University of Chicago, 1988.

Fawcett, Arthur. *The Cambuslang Revival: The Scottish Evangelical Revival of the Eighteenth Century*. London: Banner of Truth Trust, 1971.

McNemar, Richard. *The Kentucky Revival or a Short History of the Late Extraordinary Outpouring of the Spirit of God in the Western State of America*. New York, 1846.

Schmidt, Leigh Eric. *Holy Fairs: Scottish Communions and American Revivals in the Early Modern Period*. Princeton: Princeton University, 1989.

Stone, Barton W. *The Autobiography of Elder Barton Warren Stone*. Ed. John Rogers. Cincinnati, 1847.

_____. "History of the Christian Church in the West." *Christian Messenger* 1 (February 24, 1827), 74-79.

_____. *Christian Messenger* 5 (1831), 166.

Chapter 3

The Only Hope for Unity

*We may take the Bible alone, without note or
comment, as the only standard of faith and
practice, yet without the Spirit, union can never
be effected, nor continued.*

—Barton Stone

I n 1848 John Winebrenner published a book entitled *History
of All the Religious Denominations in the United States*. It
consisted of statements of belief from 53 different
American denominations. Among them was a treatment of
the "Disciples of Christ" by Robert Richardson, associate
editor of Alexander Campbell's journal the *Millennial
Harbinger*.

Some readers found Winebrenner's book disturbing.
One who did was John W. Nevin, a theologian in the German
Reformed Church. After surveying the book's 53 groups,
Nevin noted that most of the groups held one basic thing in
common: the claim to possess "no creed but the Bible." This
claim, he concluded, was the characteristic feature of
American religion in the first half of the nineteenth century.

Such a phenomenon puzzled and disturbed Nevin.
What should one think of this motley and cantankerous group

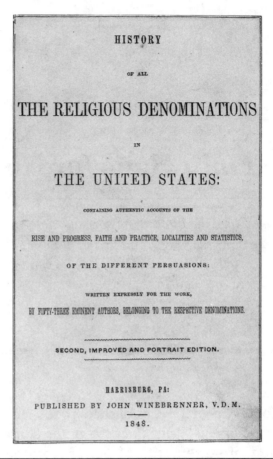

HISTORY

OF ALL

THE RELIGIOUS DENOMINATIONS

IN

THE UNITED STATES:

CONTAINING AUTHENTIC ACCOUNTS OF THE

RISE AND PROGRESS, FAITH AND PRACTICE, LOCALITIES AND STATISTICS,

OF THE DIFFERENT PERSUASIONS:

WRITTEN EXPRESSLY FOR THE WORK,

BY FIFTY-THREE EMINENT AUTHORS, BELONGING TO THE RESPECTIVE DENOMINATIONS.

SECOND, IMPROVED AND PORTRAIT EDITION.

HARRISBURG, PA:
PUBLISHED BY JOHN WINEBRENNER, V. D. M.

1848.

The title page of John Winebrenner's book surveying 53 different Christian groups. A reviewer noted that most of the groups claimed to follow "no creed but the Bible."

of sects all claiming to follow nothing but the Bible? "If the Bible be at once so full a formulary of Christian doctrine and practice," he asked, "how does it come to pass that where men are left most free to use it this way... they are flung asunder so perpetually in their religious faith?"

On the one hand, people claimed to follow "no creed but the Bible" and promised unity on that foundation; yet on the other hand, such claims and promises seemed only to multiply denominations endlessly.

Behind this fragmentation lay a profound transformation in American culture. It was an age of democratic ferment, a time when people were rising up against traditional authorities. Whether kings or clerics, exalted lords or learned theologians, people rebelled against them all. People increasingly claimed the right to interpret the Bible for themselves. The final measure of truth became, as Nevin put it, "the exercise of the single mind separately considered." The result was a sea of sects all claiming to possess nothing but the primitive faith and practice.

Richard McNemar, a reforming colleague of Barton Stone who later joined the Shakers, captured this freewheeling, fragmenting spirit in a poem:

> Ten thousand Reformers like so many moles
> Have plowed all the Bible and cut it [in] holes
> And each has his church at the end of his trace
> Built up as he thinks of the subjects of grace.

With his anti-creedal reforming movement, Barton Stone had launched out upon this sea in the opening years of the century. As years passed he saw the strife and division escalate. He heard the bold claims to simple and exclusive truth, yet saw the sad realities that belied those claims.

Stone increasingly deplored what he called the spirit of "partyism." This spirit, he said, encouraged "heresy-hunting preaching"—a practice that he viewed as one of the great cancers in the Christianity of the day.

Stone, unlike Alexander Campbell, avoided religious debates because he believed that they appealed to people's carnal desires and created ever more divisions. Their effect, he said, was to "deaden piety, destroy the spirit of prayer, puff up the vain mind, annihilate the taste for the marrow and fatness of the living word, and destroy the comforts of true, heavenly religion." Very few people, Stone felt, possessed enough Christianity to engage in debates.

Further, in Stone's view, heresy involved not so much believing wrong doctrines but a lack of love and a rending of the body of Christ. He did not believe that a set of correct doctrines would ever unite believers.

What, then, was the basis for unity? Writing in 1833, Stone said that over twenty-five years earlier he had spoken of four different approaches. The first he called "Book Union." This approach relied on the authority of creeds. It said, accept our particular creed and we will be united. But in reality such an approach produced only more division.

The second approach Stone called "Head Union." This approach rejected all creeds and boasted of taking the Bible alone. Unity would result, it was claimed, when sincere believers agreed on what the Bible teaches. But, Stone said, sincere believers do not agree on what the Bible teaches, and so they end up making their opinions the basis for unity. "Each one believes his opinion of certain texts to be the very spirit and meaning of the texts—and that this opinion was absolutely essential to salvation."

Then what difference is there, he asked, between such opinions and a creed? None at all, he replied, except that a creed is written down. And if people intend to seek unity on this basis then "surely they act more wisely who have their creed put in a book." He thus concluded that it is better to have written creeds than unwritten opinions that carry the authority of creeds. "This plan of uniting on opinions," he stated, "whether contained in a book, or in the head, is not worth a straw, and never can effect christian union, or the union of primitive Christianity."

The third approach to unity he called "Water Union." By this Stone meant a unity founded on the doctrine of immersion of believers in water. Such a union, he said, is "easily dissolved." Agreement on the doctrine of baptism simply will not keep believers united.

For Stone the only hope for unity lay in a fourth

Barton W. Stone (1772–1844): *"Fire effects a perfect union—so does the spirit of burning, the spirit of Jesus; and no union but this will stand."*

approach—what he called "Fire Union." By this he meant the fire of the Holy Spirit by which hard and unloving hearts were softened and filled with a supernatural love. "Fire effects a perfect union," he said, "—so does the spirit of burning, the spirit of Jesus; and no union but this will stand, no other union is worth the name."

Stone was convinced that schemes and plans of union were of little avail, indeed, that they easily became a source of more division. He wrote in 1831 that "a formal union on the

Bible, without possessing the spirit of that book" would be "a stumbling block, a delusive snare to the world." Seeking unity primarily on that basis, he thought, usually proved a hindrance to the quickening, sanctifying work of the Spirit. "Men have devised many plans to unite Christians—all are vain. There is but one effectual plan, which is, that all be united with Christ and walk in him."

"The great secret," he urged, "... has been almost forgotten. It is the indwelling of the Holy Spirit in each believer and member of the church." The "want of this spirit" is the "grand cause of division"; "this spirit restored will be the grand cause of union." With this Spirit, he continued, "partyism will die—without it anti-partyism in profession only, will become as rank partyism as any other, and probably more intolerant."

Stone said that he once thought that the "Bible would unite the sects." But he soon came to believe that it would not work, because "none but those who have the spirit of the Bible can really unite on the Bible." "We may take the Bible alone, without note or comment, as the only standard of faith and practice," he wrote, "yet without the Spirit, union can never be effected, nor continued." One might as well try to unite iron and clay or fire and water.

"Let every Christian begin the work of union in himself," he admonished. "Wait upon God, and pray for the promise of the Spirit. Rest not till you are filled with the Spirit. Then, and not till then, will you love the brethren... [only] then will you have the Spirit of Jesus to love the fallen world."

"O! for a revival of God's own work in the world!" he often exclaimed. "May all that profess the name of Jesus be filled with the Spirit, and bring forth the fruits of love, joy, peace, long suffering, gentleness, and goodness. Amen."

Stone believed that unity was the work of God, not of human beings. Faced with a sea of sects all claiming "no creed but the Bible," unity would emerge only as the Holy Spirit worked in human hearts, instilling in them a love divine and thereby transforming people into God's new creation.

Selected Sources

Epigraph: Stone, *Christian Messenger* 10 (1836), 30.

Hatch, Nathan O. *The Democratization of American Christianity.* New Haven: Yale University, 1989.

Stone, Barton W. "Christian Union." *Christian Messenger* 3 (December 1828), 37-38.

_____. "The Retrospect." *Christian Messenger* 7 (October 1833), 314-16.

_____. "Union." *Christian Messenger* 5 (August 1831), 185.

_____. "The Union of Christians." *Christian Messenger* 11 (March 1841), 232-38.

_____. "Union of Christians. Lecture IV." *Christian Messenger* 11 (June 1841), 334.

_____. "To Young Preachers." *Christian Messenger* 12 (1842), 316-20.

Chapter 4

Your Daughters Shall Prophesy

*The excluding of female gifts from the Church of God …
I view, as an occasion of great provocation, and as one
principal means of immense loss to the Church of the
Lord Jesus, throughout.*

—Nancy Towle (1833)

In 1812 a woman named Nancy G. Cram (1776-1815) began a teaching ministry among the Oneida Indians of New York. The Indians treated her well but she did not meet with great success. After a short time she moved on to Charleston, New York, to the home of her brother.

In Charleston Cram attended a funeral one day. At the close of the preacher's sermon she knelt and led an unscheduled prayer which deeply touched the audience. "Many wept," someone reported, "while an awful sense of eternal things seemed to settle down on the entire audience."

When the people learned that Cram was a preacher, they invited her to hold a revival meeting. Crowds gathered in barns and fields to hear her. A great revival occurred: "hundreds were soundly converted from sin, and the moral life of the community greatly increased."

When the new converts wanted to begin a church, Cram, who was not ordained, searched for an ordained Freewill Baptist minister to organize the church and administer the ordinances. Unable to find one, she traveled to Woodstock, Vermont, where she found three ministers associated with Elias Smith's "Christian" movement who were willing to come to Charleston and organize the new church.

The evangelistic success in Charleston launched Cram's highly successful four-year preaching ministry throughout New England. Great crowds attended her revival meetings. In 1814 David Millard, who became a prominent preacher in the New England "Christian" movement, was converted under her preaching. At least seven active preachers in the "Christian" movement, Millard later recalled, had been converted under her influence.

In the fall of 1815 Cram returned to her hometown of Weare, New Hampshire, where, after a sudden and brief illness, she died. She was 39 years old.

Nancy Cram was one of the most successful and well-known of Elias Smith's "female preachers." From the days of James O'Kelly in the 1790s to Smith in the early 1800s, women quietly were appointed to preach in the eastern branch of the restoration movement. Among these "female laborers," as they usually were called, were Cram, Abigail Roberts, Ann Rexford, Sarah Hedges, Clarissa Danforth, and Sally Thompson.

Abigail Roberts (1791-1841) was converted by Nancy Cram, and began a twelve year preaching ministry in 1816. She preached in out-of-the-way places, often every day for weeks at a time. She is reported to have converted hundreds and to have established at least four congregations. Bitter opposition often beset her. In one community a woman told her husband that if he would seize the "female preacher" and gag her then she would tar and feather her.

Abigail Roberts (1791–1841): one of the Smithite "female preachers."

Roberts not only bore the odium of being a woman but also of being part of Smith's "Christian" movement. In doctrine the "Christians" were labelled heretics; in social standing they were called "trash traps." Like others in the movement, Roberts preached that "party names" were wrong, that creeds usurped Christian freedom, that Christ's followers should be called simply "Christians," and that they should accept no creed but the Bible.

Elias Smith's restoration movement had begun when he broke with the Baptists about 1803 and established a

"Church of Christ" at Portsmouth, New Hampshire, noting that "we agreed to consider ourselves Christians, without the addition of any unscriptural name." The same year he met Abner Jones, also a former Baptist, and the two became leaders of a loose association of churches calling themselves the Christian Connection.

Protest against all religious tyranny and a call for "gospel liberty" lay at the heart of Smith's reform movement. A prime vehicle for these ideas was his bimonthly newspaper, *The Herald of Gospel Liberty* (1808-1817), the first religious newspaper published in America. Smith launched a crusade for a simplified Christianity, one shorn of all creeds, hierarchical authority, and clergy. "Let us be republicans indeed!" he exhorted. "Venture to be as independent in things of religion, as those which respect the government in which you live."

Smith's iconoclastic message and scorn for social conventions disturbed many people. The guardians of order, orthodoxy, and respectability thought he was "stirring up the people to revolt" and "turning the world upside down."

In 1815 Gilbert McMaster, a Presbyterian minister in New York, published a book attacking Smith and his "female preachers." He found many things about Smith offensive—the rough denunciation of Calvinism, the rejection of classical trinitarianism, the dismissal of creeds, and, not least, the sanction of women as preachers. Smith, he charged, was a "leader in heresy."

McMaster noted that Smith had "engaged a variety of characters in his service, male and female," and that Nancy Cram was one of the most notorious. He wrote that Cram was "remarkable, neither for that delicacy of mind, which is the ornament of her sex, nor for that information and good sense, by which so many of them are characterized." He added that she was "abundantly gifted with that spirit of her head, which opposes literature, order, and whatever christians usually have considered, as of vital importance to the interests of religion....she never studies, and compliments her Maker with being the author of her crude invectives."

Many people, McMaster reported with alarm, were falling victim to "the seductive address of the female heralds of *Smithite christianity*." The very use of women preachers, McMaster charged, revealed "the state of unblushing impudence at which mankind may arrive." Proper citizens should be distressed to see women "abandon the restraints and safety" of the home and become "the strolling associate of men," for such behavior was nothing less than an "outrage against social relations and the order of the church of God."

Many leaders of the established churches shared this view. By the 1830s several denominations had issued "pastoral letters" censuring women who sought public roles and who "so far forget themselves as to itinerate in the character of public lecturers and teachers."

But the conversion experience often emboldened women to step over the boundary lines drawn by social convention and to claim a higher authority. Women began to read scripture for themselves, to listen to the voice of God in their own hearts. And if the divine will as they discerned it ran counter to cultural dictates about woman's sphere or counter to the male authority in their lives, the divine will, they insisted, must take precedence.

Thus some women took the bold step of flouting the wills of their fathers and husbands, and of seeking to instruct and convert their menfolk. They organized their own religious and social reform societies. And sometimes they heeded the call to preach the gospel and evangelize the unconverted. The conversion experience, in short, provided women a "release from the prior restraints of culture or class, role or stereotype." It provided a generally accepted outlet for challenging male dominance.

Nancy Towle, a young New Hampshire schoolteacher,

provides a good example. In 1818, at age 22, she was converted under the preaching of Clarissa Danforth and baptized by Elder Moses Howe. Afterward she felt "a longing desire, to go 'into all the world and preach the Gospel to every creature.' In imagination, I was there; and in dreams of the night, I was there, sounding salvation to the thoughtless thousands."

For two years she struggled with this desire, but found no support among family and friends. "Friends became alarmed for me," she wrote. They told her that she was ruining herself; they advised her to put away her Bible and divert her mind from such "melancholy themes." But she could think only of "a world lying in darkness," of people who were "daily plunging into hell." She said that she tried to blot out such thoughts and reject her call, but found it impossible.

The question as to whether women could preach the gospel, she said, had never been a "controverted point" for her. "I ever believed, that in Christ Jesus they were one, both male and female," she explained, "and that, according to both the Old and New Testaments, holy women, as well as 'holy men of God,' were wont to speak, as they were moved by the Holy Ghost (which amounts to none other... than the preaching of the Gospel)."

Finally, on April 20, 1821, she accepted the call, turning her back on family and friends. "With the fond paternal roof, I now renounce you, once and for all!—and this day, I put my hand to the Gospel Plough, never more to turn again." "O Lord God," she cried, "I appeal to thee, that for thy name's sake, and the Gospel, I make an unreserved sacrifice, this day, of all that nature once was inclined to hold dear!"

With this step, Towle became an aggressive itinerant evangelist—years later she estimated that she had traveled over 10,000 miles in a decade of preaching. Along the way she met and worked with many other women preachers.

Regarding such women, she commented: "Those females who have renounced every earthly enjoyment, for the sake of precious souls, I ever esteem the noble part of God's creation."

In her travels Towle preached in many different churches. Some turned her away because they did not allow women to speak. In one town in Pennsylvania some members of a Methodist church asked her to preach in their chapel, but the preachers would not allow it. One said, "'A woman shall not preach there.' The other returned, 'The woman can preach better than the one that does preach there!'" Towle added: "Many high-minded men, are aggravated to see a greater congregation to hear a woman, than they could gain themselves. Oh, I pity the people that must be priest-ridden, after this sort!" She ended up preaching in the courthouse to a large audience.

In one place she was told she could not speak because it was "contrary to their rules." "I was astonished," Towle reflected, "that professed christians can be so much more willing souls shall perish, than that 'the rules of their society' shall be broken."

She worked tirelessly and endured many hardships. "I have sometimes spoken, from six to eight times a week for months in succession," she wrote, "and seldom less than one hour, sometimes two hours upon the stretch....not infrequently till midnight, and in some instances till the dawn of morning." She also told how she had been "many hundred times pennyless" and often in a strange land. "How powerful must be that charm," she reflected, "to engage and to continue for a succession of years, a female in such warfare as this!"

Towle preached wherever a platform was open to her. But she always insisted that "I am still a member of no community....I wish to be free from party spirit, and to love Christians of every order." "I am accountable to no mortal, for my procedure," she proclaimed, "nor hath any human being any control over me."

The Old Mulkey Meeting House in Monroe County, Kentucky, where Nancy Mulkey served as an "exhorter."

After fourteen years of full time itinerate preaching, Towle reflected on the "growing evils" in the world. One of these evils, she said, was the "excluding of female gifts from the Church of God;—which I view, as an occasion of great provocation, and as one principal means of immense loss to the Church of the Lord Jesus, throughout." Woman has been "taught for ages, to understand herself but a *subordinate being*—unfit for such an elevated vocation, as a *teacher of righteousness*—and hence, merely *passive* in the building of the Lord Jesus. Which is, in exact contrary to the word of God." "I for one," she concluded, "wish to deliver up my life a sacrifice towards remedying these evils, and seal my testimony, as with my blood, in vindication of the rights of woman!"

If "female preachers" were fairly common in the eastern part of the early restoration movement, they were less so in the western part. One exception was Nancy Mulkey, daughter of "Christian" preacher John Mulkey in Monroe

County, Kentucky, who served as an "exhorter" in her father's congregation. "She would arise with zeal on her countenance and fire in her eyes, and with a pathos that showed the depth of her soul," a chronicler wrote, "and would pour forth an exhortation lasting from five to fifteen minutes, which neither father nor brother could equal, and which brought tears from every feeling eye. She was remarkable in this respect." Joseph Thomas, who traveled through the region in 1812 and heard her speak, wrote that "I was no little astonished at her flow of speech and consistency of ideas."

The work of "female preachers" and "exhorters," however, soon receded. The predominant cultural model of "true womanhood," which limited woman's role strictly to the domestic sphere, became the predominant model in the restoration movement (see Chapter 18). It remained so throughout the rest of the nineteenth century and into the twentieth.

Selected Sources

Epigraph: Towle, *Vicissitudes Illustrated in the Experience of Nancy Towle*, p. 252.

Brereton, Virginia L. *From Sin to Salvation: Stories of Women's Conversions, 1800 to the Present.* Bloomington, Ind.: Indiana University, 1991.

Burnett, J. F. *Early Women of the Christian Church.* Dayton, OH: Christian Publishing Association, 1921.

Grant, J. W. "A Sketch of the Reformation in Tennessee." Typescript in the Center for Restoration Studies, Abilene Christian University.

Hatch, Nathan O. *The Democratization of American Christianity.* New Haven: Yale University, 1989.

McMaster, Gilbert. *An Essay in Defense of Some Fundamental Doctrines of Christianity; including a Review of the Writings of Elias Smith and the Claims of His Female Preachers.* Schenectady, NY, 1815.

Smith, Elias. *The Life, Conversion, Preaching, Travels and Sufferings of Elias Smith.* Boston, 1816.

Thomas, Joseph. *The Life of the Pilgrim Joseph Thomas, Containing an Accurate Account of his Trials, Travels, and Gospel Labors, up to the Present Date.* Winchester, VA, 1817.

Towle, Nancy. *Vicissitudes Illustrated in the Experience of Nancy Towle, in Europe and America.* 2nd ed. Portsmouth, NH, 1833.

Chapter 5

The Comfort of the Gospel

I sprang to my feet in an ecstacy and cried out,
'Eureka! Eureka! I have found it! I have found
it!'....I saw now the evidence of remission,
which I had never seen before.

—B. F. Hall (1826)

In the early nineteenth century the typical conversion was a long, emotional, sometimes terror-filled affair. A preacher named B.F. Hall (1803-1873) told how, at age seventeen, he first awoke to the fact that he was a "hell-deserving sinner" and how he struggled to find grace. He said he prayed with great sobs and groans; he attended church services for several weeks, and even accompanied his sister to the "mourner's bench."

When that failed he "went forward at every meeting when mourners were called for." Still not receiving deliverance, he resolved never to cease the struggle until he received some token of acceptance with God. When he finally reached conversion after several weeks, his mother marvelled that he had gotten through so quickly.

For many others the agonized quest for peace with God often lasted months or even years. Jacob Creath, Jr., who became a well-known preacher in the restoration movement, told in his autobiography how he struggled and agonized for "twelve or fifteen" years. People often told him that he must be born again, but "I did not know how to do that," he said, "nor could I tell when I was born again, nor could they tell, hence I was left in darkness without a guide or a road."

This experiential view of conversion predominated in the Protestant revivalism of the early nineteenth century. Jonathan Edwards and John Wesley had shaped this understanding in the eighteenth-century evangelical revivals. Both men, though differing on key points, believed that God converted people by the immediate work of the Holy Spirit, that is, by a sovereign divine act not dependent upon any human "means" (though God might well use such means).

Further, both revivalists taught that conversion followed a basic pattern. First, the Holy Spirit stirred an initial awakening to one's dangerous spiritual condition. Second, there followed a period of distress and deepening conviction of one's utter helplessness before God. And third, one eventually experienced deliverance and the divine assurance of pardon.

Against this predominant view of conversion Alexander Campbell directed a large amount of his writings over a span of forty years. His longest running journal, *The Millennial Harbinger*, contains over 1600 pages on the Holy Spirit, much of that writing opposing what he often termed "spiritual influences" in conversion.

Campbell explained in 1837 what had compelled him to write so much on this theme:

> If I had not met with a thousand marvelous tales of miraculous conversions by new or special illuminations, appearances, visions, dreams, that left the soul as dark as midnight ...; if I had not met with many preachers ...

almost as ignorant of the Bible as they were of the Koran, telling incredible tales of what the Lord had done for them, when they could scarcely tell where the Messiah was born, or why it behooved him to die and rise again: I say, if I had not met with multitudes thus deceived and deceiving others about spiritual operations, I should never have had any controversy on this subject.

Campbell believed fervently that the dominant Protestant model of conversion opened the door to all kinds of dangerous spiritual delusions. It ran roughshod over biblical teaching, he believed, and discredited the gospel to people of reason. He thus could call it "the greatest delusion of this our age, and one of the most prolific causes of the infidelity, immorality, and irreligion of our contemporaries."

Against such a view, Campbell adamantly insisted time and again that faith arose, not from any mysterious and "insensible operation" of the Spirit, but simply from "the belief of testimony." Indeed, he insisted that "all the converting power which the Father, the Son, or the Holy Spirit now exercises upon the human mind, is in the word" and its factual testimony to the Messiah. This testimony, in turn, without any other supernatural agency, produced faith; and faith then led a person to "obey the gospel," that is, to repent of sins and be baptized for remission of sins. Reception of the Spirit then followed gospel obedience.

The doctrine of "baptism for remission," which Campbell first set forth in his 1823 debate with the Presbyterian W. L. McCalla, played a key role.

Campbell argued that the basic problem with the dominant, experiential view of conversion was that it lacked "an institution which gives a formal, sensible, and perfect remission of sins." One was left to rummage around in one's own inner experiences, deducing one's release from sin through a shaky "train of inferential reasonings." The result, he concluded, was lingering distress and uncertainty about one's relationship to God.

B. F. Hall (1803–1873): pioneer preacher who helped spread Campbell's message of "baptism for remission" among the Stonite churches.

But the "ancient gospel" provides something more secure and comforting, Campbell proclaimed. God molded the gospel in "the form of a command." The command was to be baptized. This simple act enabled every believer "sensibly to feel" the divine forgiveness and "to remember the time and place in which he was justified and born into the family of God."

Campbell emphasized further that the gospel "makes no provision for despondency." It does not require a person to "become a desponding, trembling infidel before he can become a believer." It requires no agonized waiting for the Spirit to work, no designated "anxious seat" for those under conviction. And it leaves no lingering doubts about the reality of one's experience. Rather, people can examine the testimony of the gospel message, promptly believe it, and "obey the gospel," receiving immediately the full assurance and joy of salvation.

Baptism in this way served as a formal sign and seal of forgiveness. Though making clear that Christ's blood "really washes away" sin, Campbell stressed that the institution of baptism "formally washes" it away. Baptism thus brought a certainty of forgiveness and a sense of immediate peace with God that those who had languished on the "anxious seat" simply could not know. The institution of baptism, in short, enabled one to enjoy the full comfort of the gospel.

As this message began to spread, the results were striking. In 1826 while on a trip, B. F. Hall ran across Campbell's 1823 debate. After reading Campbell's case for baptism, Hall was elated:

> I sprang to my feet in an ecstacy and cried out, 'Eureka! Eureka! I have found it! I have found it!' And I had found it. I had found the key-stone in the gospel arch...I had found the long-lost link in the chain of gospel obedience ....I saw now the evidence of remission, which I had never seen before.

Hall said that he resumed his journey the next morning a new man. "I now had a message to every body," he wrote, "the gospel message—the whole gospel." With Hall's discovery, the doctrine of "baptism for remission of sins" spread rapidly throughout the Western Reserve.

One preacher, for example, told of baptizing a seventy-seven year old man. Asked why he had never become a Christian, the man replied that he had been waiting for God to make him a Christian. The preacher said that he promptly pointed the man to the testimony of scripture and asked him to obey it. The old man replied, "Sir, I will with all my heart." He was immersed within the hour and, according to the preacher, went home rejoicing. Another man testified that, since hearing this message, reading the New Testament had become "more delightful than ever" and that "I have enjoyed more peace than in all the rest of my life."

Jacob Creath, Jr. wrote that, following his baptism, "I had a pure, a clean and good conscience, a calmness, a sweetness, and tranquility of mind." He said he had learned that much waiting was not necessary to enter God's house. One could believe in Jesus, repent of sin, be immersed, and thus "make a short story of a long journey." The same message, he admonished, "will save you from all mental agony, through which I and thousands of others were in for years, to no profit."

James Matthews, another early preacher of this message, contrasted the exhortations of many nineteenth-century evangelists with the simple instructions of the apostles. Many evangelists say to the penitent, "Pray for faith—agonize—and wait for God's good time—bring an 'experience of grace,' and then we will baptize you." But the apostles, Matthews wrote, simply told the penitent person to "believe on the Lord Jesus Christ" and to "repent and be baptized for the remission of sins."

It was this message of comfort to troubled and insecure believers, as much as anything else, that fueled the rapid growth of Campbell's movement in the 1820s and 30s and made its appeal so powerful to Protestants of early nineteenth-century America.

Selected Sources

Epigraph: B. F. Hall, "The Proud Preacher," p. 54.

Brooks, Pat. "Alexander Campbell, the Holy Spirit, and the New Birth." *Restoration Quarterly* 31 (Third Quarter 1989), 149-64.

Campbell, Alexander, and W. L. McCalla. *A Debate on Christian Baptism.* 1823.

Campbell, Alexander. "Ancient Gospel—No. II." *Christian Baptist* 5 (February 5, 1828), 167.

_____. *The Christian System.* Bethany, VA, 1839. [pp. 39-42, 161-71]

_____. "Mr. Lynd on the Influence of the Holy Spirit." *Millennial Harbinger*, new series 1 (September 1837), 410.

Creath, Jacob, Jr. "Autobiography" (1861). Manuscript in Disciples of Christ Historical Society, Nashville, TN.

Hall, B. F. "The Proud Preacher: The Autobiography of B. F. Hall." Typescript in Disciples of Christ Historical Society, Nashville, TN.

Matthews, James E. "The Gospel Plan of Saving Sinners, No. 1." *Christian Messenger* 3 (April 1829), 125-29.

Williams, D. Newell. "The Gospel as the Power of God to Salvation: Alexander Campbell and Experimental Religion." In *Lectures in Honor of the Alexander Campbell Bicentennial, 1788-1988.* Nashville: Disciples of Christ Historical Society, 1988.

Chapter 6

The True Measure of Fellowship

If our faith be ever so imperfect, and blended with error, yet if it leads us to do the will of God, and bear fruits of the Spirit; if it works by love; if it purifies the heart; if it overcomes the world—it is the faith of a Christian.

—Barton Stone (1827)

The overflow crowd in the modest Lexington church building sat at rapt attention. Excitement mounted. The moment that many of the people had worked and prayed for drew near.

"God has but one people on earth," speaker John Smith was saying. "He has given them but one Book, and therein exhorts and commends them to be one family." Smith then recounted briefly the growing spirit of fellowship between the two groups present—between those who looked to Barton Stone and called themselves simply "Christians" and those who looked to Alexander Campbell and called themselves "reformers" or "disciples."

Stained glass window depicting the union of the Disciples and the "Christians" on January 1, 1832.

"Let us, then, my brethren," Smith concluded, "be no longer Campbellites, or Stonites, New Lights or Old Lights, or any other kind of lights, but let us come to the Bible, and to the Bible alone, as the only book in the world that can give us all the light we need."

Deeply moved by the occasion, Barton Stone stepped to the platform to respond. He spoke with fervor and joy. "I have not one objection to the ground laid down by Brother Smith as the true scriptural basis of union among God's people; and I am willing, now and here, to give him my hand."

The two men turned to face each other and shook hands. The audience burst into a hymn of celebration. The date was January 1, 1832. On the following Lord's day the two groups shared the Lord's supper together as a symbol of their unity.

The declaration of unity at Lexington was a bold and triumphant event. Many years later when Stone looked back across the span of his career, he pointed to this event as the high point. "This union," he said, "I view as the noblest act of my life."

But one would be quite mistaken to assume that the two groups declared their unity only after having resolved their significant doctrinal differences. Far from it.

The correspondence between Alexander Campbell and Barton Stone, in the years both before and after the union, reveals sharp tensions. They differed on numerous major issues: the proper name for the movement, the work of the Holy Spirit in conversion, the importance of baptism, the frequency of the Lord's supper, church government, the meaning of atonement, the doctrine of the trinity, and other matters. Because of these differences, Campbell viewed Stone's "Christian" movement as falling short of New Testament standards and thus as inferior to his own movement. For this reason Campbell, especially, had been reluctant to seek union.

The question of baptism was an especially significant point of tension between them. Both men believed that scripture taught baptism by immersion for the remission of sins. But they disagreed on whether one should allow formal fellowship with the unimmersed. Stone said yes. Campbell said no.

Stone said yes to fellowship with the unimmersed because his basic concern was Christlikeness, the possession of a "Christian spirit." "As the seal or signet, impressed on wax, leaves the image of itself," he wrote in a typical statement, "so the spirit of Christ as a seal, leaves its own image on the heart of every believer. By this we are to know that we are children of God."

Stone focused, much more than did Campbell, on the Gospels and the Sermon on the Mount. To him the test of a person's standing before God was much more ethical than doctrinal, much more spiritual than formal. And so he spoke often of "practical Christianity," of a "reformation of Christian character," and of "practical piety." He focused more on restoring the primitive holiness of life than on Campbell's restoration of the primitive order.

Character, not formal orthodoxy, he felt, provided the truest measure of a person's Christian standing. "How many, reputed orthodox, have not the mark of God's people!" he could ask, "and how many, reputed heterodox, have it so evident, that all may see it!" For Stone the true marks of a converted life were a "warm soul, tender compassion, and a spirit of love and power."

In the mid to late 1820s, under Campbell's influence, Stone began to place greater stress on "baptism for remission." He published in 1827 a series of articles on the subject by James Matthews, and they caused a sensation among the "Christian" churches. The same year Stone wrote that "faith and baptism are the divinely instituted means of salvation. The apostles preached the gospel, the people believed, and were baptized; and through these means they were saved." "This is the plan of heaven," he added.

After 1827 this doctrine spread rapidly among the Stonite churches, so that by 1830 someone reported that in Ohio 72 "Christian" preachers held this view while only 11 opposed it. By 1832 John Smith could write that the "Christian" churches had not received any members without immersion for several years.

Though upholding this doctrine, Stone would not make it a test of Christian fellowship. In his writings after

1831 he gave three reasons why. First, many sincere believers had been shaped so strongly by a tradition of incorrect teaching that they could not easily overcome it. Second, many believers possessed the true spirit of obedience even though they remained ignorant on this matter. And third, to exclude all the unimmersed would exclude many exemplary Christians from centuries past.

By 1835 Stone had witnessed a growing tendency among preachers and debaters to exclude all the unimmersed from salvation. He protested. If all the unimmersed are excluded, then "I, with millions of the fairest Christian characters on earth, would be doomed to hell forever; why? Because we had not been immersed; and this we had not done, because we were ignorant of it as a duty!" "Had I such views of God's character," he concluded, "I could not serve him with cordial love."

In apostolic times, Stone frequently stressed, fellowship required agreement only on a few fundamental truths: the existence of the Father and the Son; that Jesus is the Christ; that Christ came in the flesh; that he died and rose again; and that one must believe on Jesus and obey him. "My opinion is that immersion is [the] only baptism," he stated. "But shall I therefore make my opinion a term of Christian fellowship?"

To a person who disagreed with his view of baptism, Stone wrote: "My dear brother, I feel no disposition to wrangle with you respecting our diversity of opinion on this subject; and I hope you feel the same spirit towards me. Let us love one another, and hold forth our religion, not in the belief of certain dogmas, but in good works."

In contrast to Stone, Alexander Campbell did consider baptism for remission something worth arguing over. He did insist on excluding the unimmersed from "constitutional membership" in the church and thus from formal fellowship. At the same time, however, Campbell did not necessarily exclude the unimmersed from eternal salvation. He proclaimed the necessity of baptism for remission but allowed (especially after 1835) that those who mistook the outward baptism might possess the inner baptism of the heart (see Chapter 8).

Campbell's sharp polemics on this score distressed Stone. He protested that Campbell had constructed "an authoritative creed (though not written) of one article at least, which is formed of [his] own opinion of truth." And this short creed, he insisted, "would exclude more Christians from union than any creed with which I am acquainted."

As late as 1840 Stone pled with Campbell to "soften the hard objectionable features" of his position because they were building a wall and driving sincere people away. Further, reflecting on his travels among the churches, Stone added: "I hear much said about obedience, and too many confine or almost restrict the term to baptism and the weekly supper: prayer is sadly neglected, [along with] love to God and man."

Throughout his life, Stone sounded a common refrain, one best summed up perhaps in these words: "If our faith be ever so imperfect, and blended with error, yet if it leads us to do the will of God, and bear fruits of the Spirit; if it works by love; if it purifies the heart; if it overcomes the world—it is the faith of a Christian." He opposed the "mania for uniformity" that allowed people to exclude from fellowship those who differed in interpretation or opinion.

Despite broad and enduring doctrinal differences, and the occasional testiness of their exchanges, Stone and Campbell held each other in high esteem. They shared unquestioned fellowship in one Lord. Both sought a pure faith grounded in the Bible alone. And both abhorred division among Christians.

The remarkable union that occurred in Lexington, Kentucky, on that New Year's Day, 1832, was born of that same spirit.

Selected Sources

Epigraph: Stone, *Christian Messenger* 2 (November 1827), 5.

Campbell, Alexander. "Reply on Union, Communion, and the Name Christian." *Millennial Harbinger* 2 (September 5, 1831), 390.

Rogers, John. "To the Editors of the Christian Messenger." *Christian Messenger* 6 (April 1832), 104-105.

Stone, Barton W. *The Autobiography of Elder Barton Warren Stone.* Ed. John Rogers. Cincinnati, 1847.

_____. "The Christian Expositor." *Christian Messenger* 1 (January 25, 1827), 56-63.

_____. "Communication." *Millennial Harbinger* new series, 4 (January 1840), 21-22.

_____. "Of the Family of God on Earth." *Christian Messenger* 1 (November 25, 1826), 7-15.

_____. "Some Objections to Christian Union Calmly Considered." *Christian Messenger* 1 (December 25, 1826), 27-37.

Chapter 7

How God Works

*I see no authority in scripture, why we should
draw the conclusion, that the miraculous gift
of the Holy Spirit, is, according to the will of
God, withdrawn from the church.*

—Barton Stone (1836)

The formal union between Barton Stone's "Christians"
and Alexander Campbell's Disciples in 1832 was a
grand and surprising accomplishment. But behind the
union remained a deep, mostly hidden difference. It was not
so much a difference over this or that doctrine—though
numerous doctrinal differences remained (see Chapter 6)—
but rather a difference over the fundamental issue of how
God works in the world.

Barton Stone remained open all of his life to God's
direct, even "miraculous," working in the world, while
Campbell taught that God worked presently only through
secondary channels like natural law and the Bible.

"I see no authority in scripture," Stone wrote in an
open letter to Walter Scott in the 1830s, "why we should draw
the conclusion, that the miraculous gift of the Holy Spirit, is,
according to the will of God, withdrawn from the church."

Responding to Scott's assertion that Christians do not work miracles now, Stone asked: "Why do not some christians work miracles now? You answer correctly, because God has not given them that power. And why does he not give that power? I answer because of unbelief. If you say, because God designed that miracles should cease with the Apostles, I pray you to convince us by the testimony of the scriptures."

Near the end of his life Stone wrote a long article answering what, by that time, had become standard objections to miracles. Miracles were done to confirm scriptural truth, it was said, and thus were not necessary since the apostles' time. Stone did not agree. "What is it but a miracle to be born of God—to be made new creatures?" he exclaimed. "What but stupendous miracles will end the present dispensation?" Furthermore, "we pray God daily to perform miracles, but in unbelief of them. We pray him to protect us from our enemies, to ward off threatening casualties....If we believe he will not interpose for our deliverance, why pray for it?" Stone concluded that "the denying of miracles leads to the denying of divine Providence and interposition—and this destroys the spirit of prayer and thanksgiving."

Stone then said he had written so pointedly in order to "wake up my brethren to re-examine this subject." Because it is "a subject long neglected, and cast among the rubbish of useless divinity," he admonished, "it will require time to undo our unbelief, and the unbelief of our forefathers." "I acknowledge my faith in the doctrine is very weak," he confessed, "but my judgment declares in its favor."

Alexander Campbell held a very different view of divine agency in the world. God's power to affect people, he said many times, is "all contained in [revealed] words." Since the Bible already "contains all the arguments which can be offered to reconcile man to God, and to purify them who are reconciled," therefore "all the power of the Holy Spirit which can operate on the human mind is spent." Being filled with the Spirit basically meant filling one's mind with the words of the Bible. Thus the basic difference between the "natural man" and the "spiritual man," for Campbell, was that the first possessed only the five senses as an avenue to knowledge while the second possessed the Bible in addition.

In regard to prayer's petitions, Campbell said emphatically, one must not expect that "the laws of nature are to be changed, suspended, or new-modified, or that we are to become the subjects of any supernatural aid in obtaining these things." He affirmed divine providence but defined it simply as the "power of circumstances"—"no new miracles are wrought, no new laws or impulses are created."

These profound differences over how God works in the world point to another major difference between Barton Stone and Alexander Campbell. Stone was very skeptical about human ability to engineer progress, while Campbell had great confidence in human progress.

Stone looked with deep suspicion upon those who thought that humankind's spiritual malady was swiftly cured and that the world, as a result, was getting better and better. To the contrary, he thought, the world was growing steadily worse despite the best human exertions. The world was full of "spiritual drunkenness" and corrupt traditions and such corruption constantly fouled the machinery of progress. Only divine intervention could finally restore God's original intention for life on earth.

In Campbell's view, however, the world was progressing, not regressing. Things were getting better and better. One basic reason was that science was on the march. And as science ran its inexorable course, he said, it would gradually "exalt man above himself, and raise a generation of intellectual and moral giants from the pygmies of the present day." And when his own "restoration of the ancient gospel and order of things" was joined with this great scientific progress, then the future, he felt, appeared bright indeed.

Drawing of a camp meeting revival service in the early nineteenth century. Barton Stone looked with favor upon such meetings, while Alexander Campbell deeply disapproved.

Corrupt religion and immorality would gradually diminish and the whole earth would be "enlightened with knowledge, scientific, political, and religious."

Indeed, Campbell viewed modern history as a series of gradual, ordered, progressive steps toward a perfect or near-perfect world order—what he termed the millennial age. Thus he could write, in a well-known line, that "Just in so far as the ancient order of things, or the religion of the New Testament, is restored, just so far has the Millennium commenced."

Stone's and Campbell's contrasting views of conversion provide insight here. In Barton Stone's view, conversion involved a profound spiritual transformation wrought in the believer by the direct power of the Holy Spirit. "Without the reception of this sealing, quickening spirit through faith," he wrote, "religion is but a dream."

For this reason Stone always looked favorably on revivalism (see Chapter 2). Stone, for example, was willing, as late as 1832, to retain the "mourner's bench," a designated place where people convicted by the preaching of the gospel came to grieve over their sins and await the experience of divine forgiveness. If such a practice was "contrary to the letter and spirit of the gospel," he said, then "we cannot conceive how God should have blessed so many in the practice of it."

Stone rejected Campbell's view that in conversion the Spirit worked only through the words, facts, and arguments of the Bible. Late in his life, addressing those who held Campbell's view, Stone asked, "Will all the arguments found in the Bible ever subject the carnal mind to the mind and will of God?" He answered that the "'carnal mind is not subject to the law of God, and neither indeed can be.' Nothing less than the spirit of life in Christ Jesus can do this work; this is to be born of the spirit." Then he added: "Thousands we fear are stopping short of this by their vain philosophy, and fear of mystery, taking conversion by the word for being born of the Spirit." This might be the reason, he thought, why so many believers bore so little fruit to the glory of God.

Stone eventually came to put more stress on baptism as an outward act associated with conversion. He could say, with Campbell, that baptism indeed signified a "change of state," but he considered baptism an outward formality of lesser importance than did Campbell. For Stone, the transformation of the heart wrought by the Spirit was the key thing.

Campbell, on the other hand, held a much more rational or intellectual view of conversion. He found revivals with their experiential conversions revolting. People, he urged, could bypass all the emotional paraphernalia of revivalism when they became Christians. They could simply examine the biblical testimony, promptly believe it, and "obey the gospel," receiving immediately the full assurance of salvation (see Chapter 5).

For Campbell, conversion did not involve, as in much classical Protestantism, a sudden and dramatic change of "affections." Rather, one entered a new state or legal standing before God; change of "affections" then gradually followed the acceptance of gospel "facts." For him, God's work on the human heart was not direct but always mediated by the words of scripture and by Christ's ordinances (like baptism).

These contrasting views of how God works in the individual correlate with differing views of how God works on the large stage of human history.

Thus, if one viewed conversion as arising out of seasons of affliction and spiritual struggle, as Stone tended to do, then one's view of God's work in history tended to reflect apocalyptic images of overturning and intervention. Evil would appear more entrenched and powerful. Human effort would seem weak and insufficient. The heralds of progress would sound hollow, even deluded.

But if one viewed conversion as pre-eminently intellectual, quick, and largely free of affliction, as Campbell tended to do, then one tended to see a progressing world, one surging forward to an ever brighter future. Evil would appear to be in retreat. Progress would appear all but certain before a conquering rationality. Optimism about human potential would soar.

Stone thus saw a world stalemated by human pride and willfulness, deluded by claims to progress, and desperately needing God's dramatic intervention to set it right. Campbell thus saw a progressing world in which science, joined with a restoration of the "ancient order," gradually would usher in a new world order.

By the late 1820s Stone could write that "popular estab-

lishments must fall in order to prepare the way of the Lord."
God will "overturn, and overturn, and overturn, till Messiah
shall reign alone." In Christ's first coming, Stone said, "he
abode but a few years on earth; in his second coming he will
abide 1000, and not leave the world, till he [has]... assigned
to each one his eternal portion." In 1833 Stone wrote that
when Christ returns the saints who are alive will be changed
from mortal to immortal "and reign with the Lord on the
earth 1000 years—this is the first resurrection. The second
resurrection is of the wicked, which shall take place after the
1000 years are finished."

Alexander Campbell viewed a steadily progressing
unity as the means to usher in the millennial age of harmony
on earth. But Barton Stone thought differently. He envisioned
a dramatic, divinely-wrought millennium as the only means
to any lasting unity among believers.

Closely tied to these differences between Stone and
Campbell was a strikingly different way of understanding
Christian discipleship in the world. For Stone, Christians
lived with a deep sense of alienation from their surrounding
culture. They must separate themselves from the world with
its fashion and allures. They must be willing to surrender all
"worldly gain" and to "be stigmatized as weak—to be
accounted as fools."

Furthermore, Christians should remain uninvolved
in all politics. Human governments had arisen, Stone believed,
when human beings rebelled against God's government;
consequently, all governments stood as vestiges of the human
revolt against the divine sovereignty. Because Christians have
submitted to the rightful ruler and to his kingdom, Stone
wrote, we "must cease to support any other government on
earth by our counsels, co-operation, and choice." For Stone
this meant no political office-holding, complete pacifism, and
even refusal to vote.

Campbell, in sharp contrast, possessed little basic sense

of alienation from his culture. In the early years of his career he did lampoon expensive church buildings and oppose monied religious societies, but he eventually left such rhetoric well behind.

For Campbell, the true church was identified primarily by its correct apostolic forms and ordinances, not primarily by the visible transformation produced in the lives of believers by the Holy Spirit. Furthermore, he embraced the belief—common in his day—that the gospel and Anglo-Saxon culture formed a happy marriage and that together, in the not-too-distant future, they would triumph over the world.

For this reason Campbell could write late in his life that "There is now no cross under our [American] government. In other words there is no persecution in our country....Hence no man in these United States has to carry a cross for Christ's sake."

When the two movements united in 1832, the fundamental difference over how God worked in the world remained obscure and hidden. The "Christians" and Disciples could unite believing that they shared the same basic theology and goals. After all, both rejected creeds and sought Christian unity through a restoration of primitive Christianity. But beneath this common agenda lay two strikingly different views of how God works in this world.

Alexander Campbell's view overwhelmingly triumphed in the movement. Barton Stone's soon receded and entered the "hidden history."

Selected Sources

Epigraph: Stone, *Christian Messenger* (1836), 13.

Campbell, Alexander. "Dialogue on the Holy Spirit—Part 1." *Millennial Harbinger* 2 (July 4, 1831), 295-296.

_____. "M'Corkle Reviewed—No. 4." *Millennial Harbinger* 7 (April 1836), 159-61.

_____. "On Prayer and Special Influence." *Millennial Harbinger* 4 (May 1833), 233.

_____. "Opinionisms—No. 1." *Millennial Harbinger* 5th series, 2 (August 1859), 436-37.

_____. "Prayer—No. 1." *Millennial Harbinger* 2 (October 1831), 471.

Davidson, James West. *The Logic of Millennial Thought*. New Haven: Yale University Press, 1977.

Hughes, Richard T. "The Apocalyptic Origins of the Churches of Christ and the Triumph of Modernism." *Religion and American Culture* 2 (Summer 1992), 181-214.

Phillips, George R. "Differences in the Theological and Philosophical Background of Alexander Campbell and Barton W. Stone." Ph.D. diss., Vanderbilt University, 1968.

Stone, Barton W. *Christian Messenger* 14 (1844), 80-83.

_____. [Letter to Walter Scott]. *Christian Messenger* 7 (1836), 13-14.

_____. "The Millennium." *Christian Messenger* 7 (October 1833), 314.

_____. [Reply to a letter]. *Christian Messenger* 7 (December 1833), 365-67.

_____. "Missionaries to Pagans." *Christian Messenger* 14 (1844), 362-67.

Chapter 8

Who Is a Christian?

It is the image of Christ the Christian looks for and loves; and this does not consist in being exact in a few items, but in general devotion to the whole truth as far as known.

—Alexander Campbell (1837)

In mid-July of 1837 a brief letter from a Christian woman in Lunenburg County, Virginia, arrived in the editorial office of Alexander Campbell's journal the *Millennial Harbinger*. Campbell received scores of letters each month, many from friends, many others from foes. For some reason this letter stood out.

"Dear brother Campbell," the letter began. "I was much surprised today, while reading the *Harbinger*, to see that you recognize the Protestant parties as Christian. You say, you 'find in all Protestant parties Christians.'" Clearly puzzled and disturbed, she wanted to know how Mr. Campbell could consider anyone a Christian who had not been baptized by immersion for the remission of sins.

Campbell's answer touched off a mid-sized storm in the movement he had done so much to begin. "But who is a Christian?" he began. "Every one that believes in his heart that Jesus of Nazareth is the Messiah, the Son of God; repents of his sins, and obeys him in all things according to his measure of knowledge of his will." "I cannot," he added, "make any one duty the standard of Christian state or character, not even immersion."

His reply troubled and even shocked many people who had rallied around "the ancient gospel and order of things." Letters of protest poured in. Had not Campbell himself taught them the doctrine of baptism for remission of sins? Had he not for years done battle with the Baptists, Methodists, and Presbyterians on this very issue? Protesters felt that he was now neutralizing the doctrine and thus knocking out a vital piece of "artillery" in the movement's engagement with the Protestant world.

Why did Campbell say these things in 1837? And why were some people who looked to him as their leader so upset?

To understand this episode and its tensions we must go back to the early days of Campbell's movement. He had first set forth the doctrine of "baptism for remission" in his 1823 debate with the Presbyterian W. L. McCalla. In that debate Campbell argued for the essentiality of baptism, but at the same time made a subtle distinction—a distinction between formal and real remission. Faith in the blood of Jesus brought real remission of sins, he said, while baptism brought formal remission. And real remission, he allowed, could occur before formal remission—thus allowing for recognition of Christians who had not been immersed.

In the immediate years that followed, Campbell often did not maintain this subtle distinction. Caught up in sharp polemics, he usually sounded a simpler, louder note. He proclaimed, for example, that in Scripture "no person was said to be converted, or to turn to God, until he was buried in and raised up out of the water." Putting it even more strongly, he could say that those who did not obey the command to be baptized for the remission of sins "were not in the kingdom of Jesus Christ" and stood "worthy of condemnation."

For many of Campbell's followers, the message was clear: all who are not "baptized for remission" simply are not Christians at all.

But by the mid 1830s Campbell's emphasis began to shift. The shift occurred, in large measure, due to the hard and controversial spirit he observed in the movement. Many times throughout 1835 he spoke of the present "crisis in our history." The crisis was brought on, he stated, by the "dogmatical, unfeeling, and snarling temper" of the many preachers who "denounce error rather than preach the gospel."

Campbell lamented "the furious zeal for orthodoxy" that he felt was draining the health of the movement. Proclaimers of the ancient gospel had become "too much addicted to denouncing the sects and representing them *en masse* as wholly aliens from the possibility of salvation." They tended to "make baptism a saviour, or a passport to heaven, disparaging all the private and social virtues of the professing public."

Campbell was distressed. "We are very tired of controversy," he sighed, "and still more of that unkind, uncourteous, and proscriptive spirit which appears to be the genius of every sectarian establishment."

It was this disturbing trend that lay behind Campbell's reply to the writer from Lunenburg County, Virginia. He felt that the movement was narrowing and hardening in ways that threatened its original goals and intentions.

So in his reply he spoke bluntly: the person who concludes that "none are Christians but the immersed, as greatly errs as he who affirms that none are alive but those of clear and full vision." Further, he insisted that there is "no occasion... for making immersion, on a profession of faith, absolutely essential to a Christian—though it may be greatly essential to his sanctification and comfort."

Alexander Campbell in his early 50's: he lamented "the furious zeal for orthodoxy" that he believed was draining the health of the movement.

With this last phrase Campbell returned to the subtle distinction he had drawn earlier in the McCalla debate. Though Christ's blood "really washes away" sin, he noted, the institution of baptism "formally washes" it away. Baptism thus serves as a formal sign and seal of forgiveness, bringing an assurance and joy of salvation that the unimmersed simply cannot experience. "The present salvation," he stated, "never can be so fully enjoyed (all things else being equal) by the unimmersed as by the immersed." (See Chapter 5 on this point.)

Who then is a Christian? Campbell answered: "Every one that believes in his heart that Jesus of Nazareth is the Messiah, the Son of God; repents of his sins, and obeys him in all things according to his measure of knowledge of his will."

Campbell then raised a hypothetical situation. What if I was forced to choose between one who agreed with me on the "essentials" and one who did not agree with me but who was more "spiritually minded and devoted to the Lord"? Faced with such a choice, he replied, "I could not hesitate a moment in giving the preference of my heart to the one that loveth most." And then he added: "It is the image of Christ the Christian looks for and loves; and this does not consist in being exact in a few items, but in general devotion to the whole truth as far as known."

Surprised by the heated reactions to this reply, Campbell felt compelled in the months that followed to write more on the subject. He insisted that he always had held the view that there were "Christians in the sects." After all, what could his frequent call, "Come out of her, my people," possibly mean, he asked, if Christians did not exist outside his own movement?

Furthermore, if there were no Christians in the "sects," he proclaimed then God's promises about an everlasting church had failed. It also would mean that many of "the brightest names on earth of the last three hundred years should have to be regarded as subjects of the kingdom of Satan." And such a conclusion he was not willing to draw.

Campbell also drew a distinction between "inward and outward Christians," noting that it was possible for those who sincerely mistook the outward baptism to possess the inward. Such believers simply would not enjoy all the "Christian privileges" in this present life. He did reaffirm, however, his conviction that faith, repentance, and baptism were necessary for "constitutional membership" in the kingdom and for the Christian's joy and comfort.

Several years later, in 1845, Campbell could write: "we do not suppose all unimmersed persons to be absolute aliens from the family of God—nor are they absolutely excluded from any participation with us in prayer or in the Lord's supper."

Thomas Campbell, Alexander's father, consistently held a similar view. In 1844, for example, he wrote an article addressed to "all our Christian brethren." He explained what he meant: "By our Christian brethren, then, we mean the very same description of character addressed in our Declaration published at Washington, Pa., in the year 1809—namely, 'All that love our Lord Jesus Christ, in sincerity, throughout the [various] churches." In an 1847 article on the importance of baptism, Thomas wrote: "You may possibly infer from these remarks that I make immersion essential to salvation. By no means: for mistakes in such cases are pardonable." God judges people, he concluded, on the basis of the "available light" they possess.

Alexander Campbell's accepting attitude toward sincere believers outside his own movement appeared fairly often in his writings. In 1827 he wrote: "All the good and virtuous in all sects belong to Jesus Christ; and if I belong to him, they are my brethren....Many, I hope, will stand on the right of the Judge in the great day, who cannot now walk on the same side of the street."

This attitude toward other believers sometimes even appeared in his sharp polemics. In 1831, for example, he was concluding a long, aggressive exchange with the prominent Baptist leader Robert B. Semple. They had differed sharply over numerous doctrinal matters—the role and purpose of baptism, the work of the Holy Spirit in conversion, and other significant issues. But Campbell didn't let it end there. "If you and I should never approximate higher to each other in our views," he concluded in 1831, "I would nevertheless still love and esteem you as a Christian—as a citizen of the kingdom of heaven."

It should not seem particularly odd that, six years later, Campbell made essentially the same point in his reply to the woman from Lunenburg County, Virginia.

Selected Sources

Epigraph: Campbell, "Any Christians Among Protestant Parties," p. 412.

Campbell, Alexander. *Christianity Restored.* Bethany, VA, 1835.

_____. "Any Christians Among the Sects?" *Millennial Harbinger* new series, 1 (December 1837), 561 ff.

_____. "Christians Among the Sects." *Millennial Harbinger* new series, 1 (November 1837), 506-508.

_____. "The Crisis." *Millennial Harbinger* 6 (December 1835), 595-600.

_____. "Any Christians Among Protestant Parties." *Millennial Harbinger* new series, 1 (September 1837), 411-13.

_____. "To an Independent Baptist." *Christian Baptist* 3 (May 1, 1826), 200-205.

_____. "The Christian Magazine." *Millennial Harbinger* 3rd series, 2 (March 1845), 137-40.

_____, and W. L. McCalla. *A Public Debate on Christian Baptism.* 1823.

Campbell, Thomas. "An Address to All Our Christian Brethren, Upon the Necessity and Importance of the Actual Enjoyment of Our Holy Religion." *Millennial Harbinger* 3rd series, 1 (May 1844), 199.

_____. "Baptism." *Millennial Harbinger* 3rd series, 4 (June 1847), 323.

Chapter 9

Room for the Spirit

> *How many professed reformers [there are], to whom
> the gospel has come "in word only," and who seem
> unable to make their way out of the cocoon of
> formalism, which enwraps them and their religion
> in perpetual immaturity!*

> —Robert Richardson (1872)

In mid-nineteenth century America, religious debates were a popular form of entertainment. As one observer remarked in 1851, "Theological champions meet with burnished swords and cut and hew each other to the wondrous gratification of their respective partisans, who gather in hundreds to these scenes of religious combat."

Leaders of the restoration movement in this period excelled at debating and controversy. Many shared Alexander Campbell's judgment that "a week's debating is worth a year's preaching." The debating emphasis produced a hard, sometimes bombastic style of preaching and teaching. It brought success in the rough-and-tumble world of denominational competition, but it also spawned bitterness and fragmentation.

Dr. Robert Richardson (1806–1876) pictured on an 1856 promotional poster for Bethany College: for many years he wrote about the need for a deeper spirituality in the movement.

In the midst of this period of controversy one man sounded a different note. His name was Robert Richardson (1806-1876). By training, Richardson was a medical doctor, but he spent much of his life teaching and working as an administrator at Bethany College. He was an intimate friend of Alexander Campbell, serving as his family physician for over thirty years and as office manager and associate editor of Campbell's *Millennial Harbinger* for nearly thirty years.

When Campbell died in March of 1866, Dr. Richardson was the one chosen to deliver the funeral sermon. He was also the one Campbell's family asked to write his biography. After three intense years of research and writing, Dr. Richardson completed the massive, two-volume *Memoirs of Alexander Campbell* in 1869, a work that remains today the major biography of Campbell.

In a time of controversy and harsh debating, Richardson was unique in stressing the things of the Spirit and the devotional life. The debating mindset, he believed, produced a deadly spiritual vacuum. The effect of doctrinal controversy was to "distract the mind, destroy love, generate dislike, jealousy, revenge, [and] foster the passions of the carnal nature." Too many people, he wrote, "are ready to argue, debate, discuss, at all times, … and will spend hours in the earnest defense of their favorite theories" but will not spend five minutes meditating "upon the character, the sayings, and perfections of Christ, or upon their own inward spiritual state."

Richardson believed that this was precisely the central problem with much of the Protestant world. Each Protestant sect had developed its distinctive doctrines and theories, encased them in creeds and confessions, then tenaciously defended them against all comers. In this way Protestantism had become one "grand doctrinal controversy."

A grave error resulted, Richardson believed. Professed Christians began to mistake completely the nature and focus of the Christian faith. They began to view it "as a belief in doctrines; as consisting in correct intellectual views… ; as having respect to the mind rather than to the heart." More and more people came to regard "a correct view of doctrine as something absolutely essential to salvation, and as having in *itself*, if not a saving efficacy, at least a meritorious orthodoxy, which will go very far toward securing acceptance with God."

Richardson saw the same tendency in the restoration movement. By the early 1840s he believed that a "heartless and superficial formalism" was overtaking the movement, and this conviction grew throughout the 1840s and 50s.

He attributed this development, in large measure, to the clandestine influence of John Locke's philosophy. Locke had been the premier English philosopher of the eighteenth century, and his influence was enormous in the young American nation. He taught that true knowledge can be gained only through the five senses—and that human "reason must be our last judge and guide in everything."

Richardson labelled the popularized form of this philosophy the "dirt philosophy." He called it that because of its insistence that God could influence human beings only through material objects or through revealed words—no other way. Such a philosophy, he frequently charged, was spiritually debilitating, for it tends to "unfit men's minds to receive anything that is not merely outward and formal"; it thereby "gradually dries up the fountains of spiritual sympathy."

In a private letter to Isaac Errett on July 16, 1857, Richardson spoke to this point with unusual candor: "the philosophy of Locke with which Bro. Campbell's mind was deeply imbued in youth has insidiously mingled itself with almost all the great points in the reformation and has been all the while like an iceberg in the way—chilling the heart and benumbing the hands, and impeding all progress in the right direction."

It was the direct influence of this "dirt philosophy," Richardson believed, that led many people in the movement to deny any significant present-day role to the Holy Spirit and thereby foster a doctrinal formalism. In reacting against the abuses of the doctrine of the Spirit in popular theology, many leaders, he believed, had become "so extremely cautious upon the subject that, so far from cultivating religious feeling, they seem rather to repress it, and to encase religion within the ices of a philosophical sensibility."

Two extreme positions attracted many people, he thought. One he called the "Spirit alone" theory, the other the "Word alone" theory. On the one hand, the advocate of the "Spirit alone" view "imagines himself to have realized the presence of the Spirit in some emotional excitement, some brilliant vision, or some audible revelation." On the other hand, the advocate of the "Word alone" view "amuses himself with the notion that he has resolved all the mysteries of the Holy Spirit, when he has persuaded himself that this Spirit is merely a visible and tangible New Testament."

Both extremes, he said, pervert scripture's plain teaching about the work of the Spirit. But if forced to choose between the two views, he said, he would certainly choose the "Spirit alone" position, for such views "at least lead the mind to seek after fellowship with God; and embody the idea... that there is a real communion to be enjoyed with the spiritual world."

Richardson recognized that some people went to emotional excess in their religion, but he felt that the opposite extreme—a Spiritless faith—was an even greater evil. And so he steadfastly opposed those, including his close friend Alexander Campbell, who tended to reduce the Spirit's influence to the Bible alone. Campbell had insisted, for example, that since the Bible already "contains all the arguments which can be offered to reconcile man to God, and to purify them who are reconciled," therefore "all the power of the Holy Spirit which can operate on the human mind is spent."

Such views, Richardson believed, retarded spiritual vitality and growth. How many professed reformers there are, he exclaimed, "to whom the gospel has come 'in word only,' and who seem unable to make their way out of the cocoon of formalism, which enwraps them and their religion in perpetual immaturity!" Limiting the Spirit's influence to the

Bible alone, he thought, "degrades the Bible, by placing it in a false position, and ascribing to it exclusive power and attributes which it never claims for itself."

Throughout his many writings Richardson called his fellow believers to a religion of the Spirit, to a faith empowered by the personal indwelling of the Holy Spirit. With Christian faith beset by worldliness, compromise, formalism, and bitter controversies, how, Richardson asked, will a vital Christian faith be restored to the world? He answered: "by returning to the primitive faith and love; by doing the first works, and by a manifestation in the life of those fruits of the Spirit which alone reveal the truth of religion, and demonstrate to the world the divine mission of Jesus."

But in order to show forth the fruit of the Spirit, Richardson quickly added, "the presence of the Spirit Himself is necessary." Indeed, in the present day the presence of the Holy Spirit in a fuller measure is the "true want of the Church." People must "return to the simple faith of primitive times, and cease forever from those discords and dissensions which ... have largely banished the Holy Spirit from the hearts" of professing Christians.

The Holy Spirit, Richardson said, is "God's missionary" to human hearts. The Spirit, he often affirmed, is "imparted to the believer, really and truly, taking up His abode in his person, as a distinct guest, or inhabitant." The Spirit is "God enthroned in man's *moral* nature, renewing and sanctifying the affections, and transforming humanity into the Divine image." The Spirit does this through "the graces it imparts and through the 'ingrafted Word' which it has introduced into the heart, and now ever preserves green in the memory and fruitful in the life."

Without the Spirit, Richardson thought, faith loses its true character, becoming more the adoption of a doctrinal system than of a spiritual life. Indeed, without the Spirit much that passes for orthodoxy is vain.

In vain do men weary themselves and the world with plans of reformation; with systems of belief; with schemes of union based on human wisdom. In vain do they imagine themselves to have discovered the secret of the power of the primitive church in its freedom from priestly rule; or in its super-natural gifts; or in any other exterior characteristic.

The secret of the early church's power was nothing less than this: "the indwelling of the Spirit of God, giving unity, imparting energy, evolving the glorious fruits of Christianity, and presenting to the world, in every disciple, an illustration of the life of Christ."

Selected Sources

Epigraph: Richardson, *A Scriptural View of the Office of the Holy Spirit*, p. iv.

Brooks, Pat. "Robert Richardson: Nineteenth Century Advocate of Spirituality." *Restoration Quarterly* 21 (1978), 135-49.

Goodnight, Cloyd, and Dwight E. Stevenson, *Home to Bethphage: A Biography of Robert Richardson*. St. Louis: Christian Board of Publication, 1949.

Richardson, Robert. "Faith versus Philosophy." *Millennial Harbinger* 4th series, 7 (1857).

_____. "Nature of Christian Faith." *Millennial Harbinger* 4th series, 6 (March 1856), 153-60.

_____. "Nature of the Christian Doctrine." *Millennial Harbinger* 4th series, 6 (April 1856), 198-204.

_____. *A Scriptural View of the Office of the Holy Spirit*. Cincinnati, 1872.

Chapter 10

The Bond of Peace

Oh! to set the heart right first saves the head a world of useless trouble, for it is truly through the heart alone that any one can comprehend the "doctrine of God."

—Robert Richardson (1856)

In 1841 representatives from 29 churches of the restoration movement met in Nashville to discuss matters of church polity and teaching. According to the report of the gathering, someone asked the question whether or not the Bible permits Christians to differ from one another.

To this question someone answered that "In the kingdom of Messiah, all the subjects are bound to think alike." "The Bible reveals every religious duty," the answerer continued, therefore differences among believers "always manifest either ignorance of the law or a determination to rebel against it." The report noted that "all agreed thereto."

In the mid 1850s, faced with upheaval and division in the Nashville church, Tolbert Fanning, founding editor of the *Gospel Advocate*, said essentially the same thing. "Everything is a subject of authority and there is no room for debate," he wrote. "We have complete instructions in all matters pertaining to religion, or we have nothing." Thus, regarding the "externals, or ordinances" of the faith, he could write that "the least change, whatever, not only annihilates them, but all genuine religion."

This viewpoint marked a considerable shift away from the movement's pioneers. The earliest leaders had envisioned a large realm of diversity in the reading of the Bible. Barton Stone, Alexander Campbell, Walter Scott, and others had said in effect, "In faith unity; in opinions liberty." This slogan, in fact, had become a frequent refrain as the movement had spread.

The early leaders acknowledged that even the most sincere and diligent believers would not agree at many points. But all could agree, they believed, on the basic facts of the gospel—the essentials that belonged to no sect or party.

But by the 1840s and 50s the realm of allowable diversity had narrowed sharply in a segment of the movement. Indeed, as we saw in Chapter 8, Alexander Campbell by the mid 1830s expressed dismay over such narrowing and the internal controversy it produced.

In this context Robert Richardson, Campbell's close friend and associate editor, began a long series of articles in 1847 entitled simply "Reformation." In 1853 he published a condensed version of the articles in a small book entitled, *The Principles and Objects of the Religious Reformation, Urged by A. Campbell and Others, Briefly Stated and Explained.* The book circulated widely. Campbell praised it, noting that it "gives a well proportioned miniature view" of the movement's original goals.

The movement rested, Richardson said, upon three basic principles. First was a distinction between faith and opinion. The movement sought to recover a core of essentials comprising a "common Christianity," thereby allowing greater room for diversity of opinion.

The Protestant churches, he said, sought to take the Bible alone, and that certainly was proper. But in their great zeal for pure doctrine they committed a serious error: they went "too much into detail," constructing elaborate confessional statements and measuring orthodoxy by agreement on a sizeable body of doctrine.

To make a proper distinction between faith and opinion, Richardson argued, one cannot simply say, "The Bible alone is our creed." For the Bible is a rich, detailed, and complex library that can occupy the greatest minds for a lifetime. Expecting people to unite by understanding it alike will simply insure continued division in the Christian ranks.

In claiming to take the Bible alone, Richardson said, many believers fail to distinguish between the Bible and the gospel. The apostles and earliest preachers had no Bibles to distribute, so "there was no such thing as a formal union upon the 'Bible alone.' Nay, rather, it was a union upon the Gospel alone."

The gospel, Richardson believed, consisted of the simple facts of Christ's death, burial, and resurrection (1 Cor. 15:3-4). This was the baseline of faith. Believers would never unite on a broad doctrinal platform—300 years of Protestant wrangling and division had proved that; but they could unite on the simple facts of the gospel.

When one received these facts into one's heart by faith, one was saved; and "that alone which saves men, can unite them." The great confession, "I believe that Jesus Christ is the Son of God," should therefore serve as the "only authorized test of orthodoxy." Beyond that, believers should allow each other much room for opinions and for growth in understanding.

"Let the Bible be our spiritual library; but let the Gospel be our standard of orthodoxy," Richardson said. "Let the Bible be our test of Christian character and perfection, but let the Christian confession be our formula of Christian adoption and Christian union." "In a word," he concluded, "let the Bible be every thing designed by its Author, but let 'Christ crucified' be not only our peace with God, but our peace with one another."

The second basic principle of the movement, Richardson said, was a distinction between "the Christian faith" and "doctrinal knowledge." What does it mean to believe in Christ? he asked. He answered that it means not simply to receive his doctrine or to believe what he says. Rather it means to be brought into *"direct relation* and *fellowship* with Him; to think of Him as a *person* whom we know, and to whom we are known." It means to speak to him and listen to him as one would to a close friend.

"Christ is not a doctrine, but a person," Richardson urged. At its heart Christian faith centers on a person, not a body of doctrines. It does not consist essentially in the "accuracy of intellectual conceptions," but rather in a certain kind of life—a transformed inner life and a fruitful outer life. People may possess "the same faith, while they differ greatly in the amount and accuracy of their religious knowledge."

The broad expanse of biblical doctrine, he carefully pointed out, must never be discounted, for it serves as an important superstructure. But it does not provide the foundation. That is found only in a deeply personal relationship with Christ—and "the foundation must precede the superstructure."

The main problem behind a fragmented Christian world, Richardson believed, is that people confuse trust in a living savior with belief in certain doctrines. When this happens faith gets "supplanted by polemics." Sectarian belligerence and rivalry mount. Doctrinal creeds, whether written or unwritten, become the basic measure of orthodoxy. And people inevitably grow distant from Christ. They grow distant, Richardson said, because a "syllabus of doctrine has no power to enlist the heart and the energies of the soul in the true work of Christ."

Indeed, what "every true sectary lacks" is this personal reliance on Christ. He stands on the walls of his camp and asks those who seek to enter, not "In *whom* do you believe?" but rather "*What* do you believe?" He thinks that the error and confusion of the human heart will be remedied by intellectual opinions.

But his way is the way of human folly. The way of divine wisdom is "to correct the errors of reason by regulating the affections." "Oh! to set the heart right first," Richardson exclaimed, "saves the head a world of useless trouble, for it is truly through the heart alone that any one can comprehend the 'doctrine of God.'"

The first two basic principles provided the foundation for the third: the restoration of "SIMPLE EVANGELICAL CHRISTIANITY" as the true basis for Christian union. Reiterating much of Campbell's original agenda, Richardson said that the movement sought to restore "the gospel and its institutions, in all their original simplicity, to the world." This, he thought, was the scriptural basis—and only hope—for the visible union of believers.

But Richardson made a significant distinction. Commenting on Jesus' prayer for unity in John 17, he distinguished sharply between unity and union. Unity, he said, referred to "a spiritual oneness with Christ," while union was "an avowed agreement and co-operation of Christians with each other."

Most interpreters of John 17, he said, mistake union for unity. They suppose that Jesus' prayer for unity has not been answered and thus expect "some future fusion of all religious parties into one, or the creation of some grand overshadowing community" of faith.

But Jesus' prayer *has* been answered, Richardson insisted. Not in a universal, visible union, of course, but in a spiritual unity. The sinful state of humankind "utterly precludes the possibility of any denominational or organic union among believers in this wide world," he said, "but the unity for which Christ prayed is always, and has been always, not only possible but existent." This unity is a spiritual oneness created by the presence of the Holy Spirit for which Christ prayed. It is not a doctrinal uniformity or an ironing out of differences, but a oneness given by joint participation in the Spirit.

Of course, Richardson said, believers should pray for visible union, for the breakdown of "the bigotry of denominationalism and the rancor of party spirit." But such a prayer is always a prayer for the Spirit and should not be "misapplied to so inferior a matter, and one so improbable, as a future universal, organic Christian union."

Late in Richardson's life a correspondent told him about a union overture with Baptists in Virginia and asked his opinion. We were part of the Baptists in the early days, replied Richardson, and have never wholly separated. There were sharp controversies, to be sure, but "at no time have we separated ourselves, or denied fellowship to a Baptist brother, or refused to receive as a member any one accredited by a letter from a Baptist church. We have, in reality, ever claimed the Baptists as our brethren."

At a time when some leaders in the movement insisted that all true Christians were "bound to think alike," Richardson held up a different vision—the one that he thought had first launched the movement. The demand for doctrinal uniformity, he believed, inevitably entangled believers in the "bonds of partyism," while only a unity in the Spirit drew them together in the "bond of peace."

Selected Sources

Epigraph: Richardson, "Nature of the Christian Doctrine," p. 204.

Fanning, Tolbert. *Gospel Advocate,* (February 1856), 42.

_____. *History and True Position of the Church of Christ in Nashville.* Nashville, 1854.

Richardson, Robert. "Christian Unity—No. I." *Millennial Harbinger* 5th series, 2 (February 1859), 64-69.

_____. "Nature of the Christian Doctrine." *Millennial Harbinger* 4th series, 6 (April 1856), 198-204.

_____. *The Principles and Objects of the Religious Reformation, Urged by A. Campbell and Others, Briefly Stated and Explained.* Bethany, 1853.

_____. "Reformation—No. IV." *Millennial Harbinger* 3rd series, 4 (September 1847), 503-509.

_____. "Union of Christians." *Millennial Harbinger* 37 (March 1866), 97-101.

Chapter 11

Holy Mysteries

*In proportion as the mysteries presented to us
deepen, they approach nearer to God. He is
the great mystery of mysteries, and we draw
nearer to Him as we approach the veil that
conceals his inner temple.*

—Robert Richardson

The modest audience in the small Bethany church
building on that Sunday morning in 1848 waited
eagerly as Dr. Robert Richardson rose from his seat,
walked slowly to the communion table, then turned to face
the congregation.

Alexander Campbell had just delivered the morning
sermon, as usual. But now the audience awaited a special
treat—a communion meditation from Dr. Richardson. These
meditations, delivered from time to time over the years, were
memorable events, and the Bethany Church of Christ—made
up mostly of students and faculty—eagerly anticipated them.

The doctor stood facing the congregation for several
moments. There was utter silence. He was a thin, dignified
man standing somewhat taller than Mr. Campbell.

The Bethany Church of Christ where Robert Richardson delivered the communion talks published in Communings in the Sanctuary.

"How truly incomprehensible and beyond comparison is the love of God for man!" he began in his high-pitched, reticent voice. "Inscrutable as his ways, unsearchable as his judgments, deep as the exhaustless mines of his wisdom and knowledge, his love but partakes of the infinitude of his nature." He paused slightly. "How, then, can we hope to fathom its depths, to estimate its value, or to realize its power!"

Richardson spoke further of the magnitude of that love and of how weak and small seem our noblest efforts in comparison. "But, alas! how shall man return a love of which he can not even adequately conceive?" he asked. "It is as high as heaven; it is vast as the universe! How can he attain to it? How can he compass it?"

These exclamations and questions point to the heart of the spiritual life as Richardson conceived it. "True religion" meant entering into spiritual union with God. It meant contemplating the divine glory and the "ever-opening mysteries of redeeming love." It meant allowing oneself to be renovated into a living temple for the Holy Spirit.

Throughout his life Richardson addressed these themes with a quiet passion and eloquence. In a time when doctrinal, polemical, and organizational matters preoccupied the movement, he remained a persistent—at times almost solitary—advocate of a deeper, richer spirituality. It was here, he felt, that the movement was most lacking. In 1842 he noted, for example, "a dull insensibility in respect to spiritual things, which seems to arise from an ignorance of there being any such thing as a true and spiritual union with God and Christ."

A few other voices had raised such concerns before him. John Rogers of Carlisle, Kentucky, for example, had written to Campbell in 1834, noting that "many of us, in running away from the extreme of enthusiasm, have, on the other hand, passed the temperate zone, and gone far into the frozen regions." "There is, in too many churches," he added, "a cold-hearted, lifeless formality, that freezes the energies."

And Campbell himself, on a few occasions, could raise such concerns. Religion certainly was an intellectual matter, he wrote in 1837, "but religion dwelling in the heart, rooted in the feelings and affections, is a living, active, and real existence." This is what fills the soul with divine life. "This is religion," he concluded; "all the rest is machinery."

Richardson picked up such concern and made it a lifelong focus. His writings resound with the call to the spiritual life. But nowhere is his vision of that life more powerful and eloquent than in his many communion meditations delivered to the Bethany church.

J. W. McGarvey was a student at Bethany College in 1847-48 and heard many of them. "The richest service of all," he later wrote, "was when they had a sermon by Mr. Campbell followed by Dr. Richardson in a five- or ten-minute talk at the Lord's table." These talks were gems of beauty, he said.

Between 1847 and 1850 Richardson published a series of the talks in the *Millennial Harbinger* under the title "Communings in the Sanctuary." Later, at the urging of McGarvey and others, he collected twenty-four of them into a small book of the same title. That book remains the first and greatest of the devotional books written in the movement.

At the heart of the book lies a constant sense of the awesome mystery of things human and things divine. Three themes predominate.

(1) *The mystery of the holy.* In Richardson's view, recognition of the divine mystery is fundamental to Christian faith. Far from hindering one's vision or obstructing one's spiritual progress, the recognition of mystery brings "truer and nobler" views of God. "In proportion as the mysteries presented to us deepen, *they approach nearer to God,*" Richardson said. "He is the great mystery of mysteries, and we draw nearer to Him as we approach the veil that conceals his inner temple."

In one of the talks, Richardson contrasted the "religion of the imagination" and the "religion of the intellect." The first, he said, focuses on nature and its beauties. To its devotees, the world becomes "an emanation from the Beautiful, which is their deity and idol." Their great error, he said, lies in thinking that true religion consists in reverence for God's beautiful creation.

But, Richardson said, a "thousand charms" mark such religion when one compares it with the "barren and undecorated religion of the intellect." For these devotees are obsessed with analyzing the organisms of the spiritual system and dissecting its outward forms—squeezing out their life and beauty in the process. In this view, Richardson says, "to *think* right is to *do* right, and to worship *reason* is to worship God."

But in the sanctuary of God, with the "Lamb that was slain" lifted up and the emblems of divine love spread, both errors find their corrective. There one can neither "bow in the chambers of imagery nor yield to the idolatry of reason." Indeed, how poor and feeble do those things seem "when the heart feels the love of God, and the soul rejoices in the Beloved!"

"Before the cross of Jesus," Richardson continued, "the magnificence of earth is vanity, and the power of intellect but pride." Before the cross one must exchange the "religion of the imagination" for the great promises of Christian hope and subject human reason to the "mysteries of Revelation." And it is a great and happy exchange. For Christian hope opens more glorious scenes than anyone can imagine and the "mysteries of Faith are more sublime than those of Reason."

In pointing to the mysteries of faith, Richardson did not cast out reason. The Christian faith contains intellectual depths, to be sure, and the mind seeks to plumb them. Reason especially plays an important role in the "preliminary examination of the facts and evidences of the gospel." But reason's power is sharply limited. It simply cannot purify the heart and bring human passions under control. Only the gospel can do that. In purifying and transforming the heart the gospel reveals its greatest power and profoundest mysteries—here one finds that "a 'deeper deep' speedily exhausts the plumb line of reason and philosophy."

(2) *The mystery of Christ's atoning death.* Because Richardson prepared these talks for the communion service, they invariably centered in Christ's death. Though the coming of Christ into the world was a great mystery, he said, "how much greater *the mystery of his death!* What new and wonderful developments it gives of the divine character! What startling thoughts it suggests of things invisible!"

So inscrutable was the mystery of the atonement, many preachers in the movement thought, that dwelling on it or trying to explore it yielded little profit. One did better to affirm the simple historical facts, then turn to more practical and understandable matters—like what people must do to be saved.

Richardson thought otherwise. To him the events of Jesus' death were "transcendent facts" full of meaning and mystery. By fixing one's eyes there, troubled consciences and rough desires were stilled by the "potent charm of Jesus' love." By entering its dark places and exploring its deeps time and again one grew ever more captivated by holy things and higher loves. Indeed, in contemplating such mysteries, one came to "see more of God than angels knew before!"

(3) *The mystery of union with God and Christ.* In Richardson's view the Christian faith was not "a mere system of salvation from sin," with the cross being one part of that system. Neither was Jesus' death simply a removal of sin's penalties. Its purpose rather was "to effect a *renovation*—a *regeneration* of the soul."

Many believers, he thought, view redemption as a kind of commodity "which they may obtain upon certain terms, of which the ministers of the Gospel are supposed to be the negotiators." But redemption is no negotiable commodity. Rather, it involves nothing less than a transforming union with God and Christ through the Holy Spirit.

This union is one of faith's great mysteries. Through it the believer develops entirely new spiritual sensibilities. As those senses are cultivated, the believer grows "as fully alive to the things of the spiritual world, as is the natural man to the things of the natural world." He develops "a fellowship with spiritual existences and objects of whose very existence he was formerly wholly unconscious." In a word, the believer becomes fit for life in heaven with God.

Standing behind the communion table on that Sunday morning in 1848 Dr. Richardson brought his talk to a close. "How shall man return a love of which he can not even adequately conceive?" he had asked.

"Oh! how joyful the reflection," he now answered, "that however weak our powers, however imperfect our efforts, the Divine Comforter can shed abroad the love of God in our hearts, enlarge our capacities, transform all our feeble nature, and render us partakers of the divine fullness."

In front of him the table was spread and ready. He looked down at it for a moment then back to the audience.

"Inscrutable and sublime mystery," he exclaimed, his voice trembling slightly, that "the glorious Being, of whom our unequal powers can form no adequate conception, and whose glory fills both earth and heaven, can yet find a dwelling place in the human heart!"

Dr. Richardson turned and walked quickly back to his seat. Servers came forward and the congregation communed together, sharing the sacred emblems of divine suffering and glory.

Selected Sources

Epigraph: Richardson, *Communings in the Sanctuary*, p. 115.

Campbell, Alexander. "The Power of Religion—No. I." *Millennial Harbinger* new series, 1 (1837), 8-10.

Goodnight, Cloyd and Dwight E. Stevenson. *Home to Bethphage: A Biography of Robert Richardson.* St. Louis: Christian Board of Publication, 1949.

Richardson, Robert. *Communings in the Sanctuary.* Cincinnati, date unknown.

_____. "Pure and Undefiled Religion—No. I." *Millennial Harbinger* 5th series, 2 (November 1859), 622-26.

Chapter 12

The Peaceable Kingdom

*The mission of the kingdom of God is to break into
pieces and consume all earthly kingdoms, take
their place, fill the whole earth, and stand forever.*

—David Lipscomb (1889)

The American Civil War broke out early in 1861 when
Union troops fired on Confederate troops at Ft. Sumter
near Charleston, South Carolina. With the outbreak of
war, the Christians of the restoration movement faced an
unavoidable question: would they remain loyal to their region
of the country and fight or would they oppose the war out of
a higher allegiance?

By the 1860s there were about 1200 congregations in
the North and about 800 in the South. Many of these churches
were located in border states such as Missouri and Kentucky,
and consequently the same congregation often included both
Union and Confederate sympathizers. Tensions ran high.
What were sincere Christians to do?

The majority of church members held pacifist views. While some leaders advocated total pacifism in all circumstances, many others argued simply that it was wrong to fight in a war in which one might well kill other Christians. Alexander Campbell, Tolbert Fanning, Moses Lard, J. W. McGarvey, Benjamin Franklin, and David Lipscomb—all of these leading preachers and many others urged Christians to stay out of the war.

J. W. McGarvey, for example, was one of several ministers who wrote to Jefferson Davis, President of the Confederacy, requesting conscientious objector status for Christians in the South. "I would rather ten thousand times be killed for refusing to fight," McGarvey wrote, "than to fall in battle, or come home victorious with the blood of my brethren on my hands." He asked Christians to consider what the apostles would have done if six had lived in the North and six in the South. "Would they, like the hosts of sectarian preachers on both sides, be urging their brethren to war?"

Among the southern Churches of Christ, David Lipscomb was emerging as one of the most influential leaders. After farming for several years in Franklin County, Tennessee, he began preaching throughout middle Tennessee in 1856. When the war began he strongly discouraged Christians from fighting, and he successfully persuaded many fellow Christians in the South to refuse military service. His pacifism was strongly reinforced when on December 15 and 16, 1864, he witnessed the Battle of Nashville in which 3,000 Union soldiers and 1,500 Confederate soldiers died.

Lipscomb spent the rest of his life opposing Christian involvement in war. Indeed, he opposed Christian involvement in all political affairs, and even taught that Christians should not vote. Through the *Gospel Advocate*, an influential weekly magazine which he edited from 1866 until 1912, he influenced many southern Christians with his views. In fact, Lipscomb was unquestionably the most influential leader

David Lipscomb (1831–1917): the most influential leader among southern Churches of Christ in the second half of the nineteenth century.

among southern Churches of Christ in the second half of the nineteenth century.

To understand Lipscomb's pacifism we must see its deep roots in his understanding of the kingdom of God. Lipscomb imbibed much of Alexander Campbell's rational and "common sense" theology, but, as Richard Hughes has pointed out in an important study, his writings also reveal an understanding of the kingdom remarkably similar to Barton Stone's.

That similarity is not surprising, for Lipscomb's earliest religious influences came out of Stone's "Christian" movement. By 1831, the year of Lipscomb's birth, his father and uncles had been expelled from the Baptist church and had united with a Stonite church. According to Lipscomb, the first preacher of the restoration movement he remembered hearing was Thacker V. Griffin at the Salem Church on Bean's Creek in Franklin County, Tennessee (a church established by the Stonite preacher James Matthews). Furthermore, Lipscomb's mentor was Tolbert Fanning, who had been deeply influenced by several Stonite preachers in his youth.

Alexander Campbell's influence, of course, also figured prominently. Lipscomb indicates something of the extent of it when he reported that he had read every issue of the *Millennial Harbinger* since he was ten years old.

But though heavily influenced by Campbell, Lipscomb maintained and developed key aspects of Stone's view of God's kingdom, an outlook largely foreign to Campbell (see Chapter 7). He published his views in scores of articles but most prominently in a small book entitled *Civil Government: Its Origin, Mission, and Destiny and the Christian's Relation to It* (1889).

Like Stone before him, Lipscomb believed that all human government represented the rebellion of humankind against God's sovereign rule and the transferring of allegiance to the kingdom of Satan. Citing the rise of Nimrod (Genesis 10:8), he said that human government began as "the organized effort of man to govern himself" and "to conduct the affairs of the world independently of the government of God." God eventually gave people their way, sanctioning civil government as a punishment for their rebellion.

As a result of this rebellion against God's government, the earth, which was once a paradise, became "a dried and parched wilderness" where sin and suffering permeated everything. Under human governments, it became a place of "confusion, strife, bloodshed, and perpetual warfare." "The chief occupation of human governments from the beginning has been war," Lipscomb said. "Nine-tenths of the taxes paid by the human family, have gone to preparing for, carrying on, or paying the expenses of war."

Christ came, Lipscomb said, to rescue this world and to restore it to its "primitive and pristine allegiance to God." Christ mightily engaged Satan's rule and succeeded in re-establishing God's kingdom. This kingdom in its present churchly form, however, was not the "everlasting kingdom" but rather the kingdom in "a lower state of growth and development."

But the time will come, Lipscomb believed, when Christ will "put down all rule, and all authority and all power." Through Christ, God's kingdom "shall break in pieces and consume all the kingdoms of earthly origin." Then Christ will deliver up the kingdom to the Father and God will rule "in and through his restored kingdom on earth."

When that occurs, Lipscomb stressed, peace will reign: "the will of God will be done on earth as it is in heaven, and all things in the world will be restored to harmonious relations with God." The earth itself, Lipscomb thought, would be transformed: "briars and thorns, material and spiritual, will no longer grow—the atmosphere will be purified of its rebellious taint and death will be destroyed—*this world* will become the Eden of happiness and peace."

How, some might wonder, would the practical affairs of human life be managed in this fully restored earthly kingdom? "How would the mails be carried?" How would transportation and manufacturing be handled? Wouldn't some kind of civil government be necessary? To such questions, Lipscomb answered that he didn't know, but that he would "cheerfully commit the adjustment and management of all things pertaining to the world" to the divine wisdom and skill.

As these quotes show, Lipscomb clearly envisioned a

restored and perfected millennial kingdom on the earth. He refused, however, to speculate about whether or not Jesus would reign over this earthly kingdom for a literal thousand years. Such a question, he thought, was among the "untaught questions" best left to God alone.

For Lipscomb, as for Barton Stone before him, this outlook deeply shaped his understanding of Christian discipleship in this present world. Christians should stand aloof from civil government, refusing to hold political offices, to participate in war, and even to vote. For how, Lipscomb asked, "could the individual citizens of the kingdom of God found, enter into, and become part and parcel of that which God's kingdom was especially commissioned to destroy?" Christians rather should stand apart, living lives of simplicity, sacrifice, and service, and expecting as a matter of course the misunderstanding and scorn of the world.

For Lipscomb, God's kingdom remained a transcendent reality that alone should claim Christians' allegiance. Because Christians were citizens of that kingdom, they placed little hope in human governments with all their might and force. God's kingdom, he believed, was a kingdom of peace and it could never be shaken—indeed, it would one day fill the whole earth.

This outlook lay at the heart of Lipscomb's theology. He summarized it most succinctly in his essay, "The Ruin and Redemption of the World," and developed it most fully in his book *Civil Government*. In 1890 he said that "nothing we ever wrote so nearly affects the vital interests of the church of Christ and of the salvation of the world as this little book."

Pacifist views like Lipscomb's remained strong among Churches of Christ until the early twentieth century. Though a good many who embraced pacifism rejected or simply did not understand the view of God's kingdom that undergirded it, Lipscomb's outlook did influence a significant circle of people.

By the time of World War II, however, Lipscomb's outlook, with its dim view of all human governments, its sole allegiance to God's kingdom, and its ardent pacifism, had eroded badly. Churches of Christ were growing increasingly at home in mainstream American culture and thus ever more content with conventional Protestant morality. With the war fever raging, the strict pacifist stance prominent in Lipscomb's time made little sense to many people.

A preacher in the movement named O. C. Lambert expressed the prevailing attitude. "I lose faith in the Lipscomb Lion and Lamb story!" he proclaimed in 1943. Indeed, Lambert stated that Churches of Christ should call in all copies of "the Lipscomb book [*Civil Government*]" and burn them. So dangerous was the book's message, he asserted, that it "would be outlawed now if the FBI knew its contents."

Another, more prominent preacher and thought leader, Foy Wallace, Jr., repeatedly attacked Lipscomb as a dangerous heretic. He charged that Lipscomb's book, *Civil Government*, was "about as rank with false doctrine as one book of its size could be." He ridiculed Lipscomb's pacifism and charged him with fostering the growth of premillennialism in the movement.

By the late twentieth century, Lipscomb's view of God's kingdom and the pacifism tied closely to it had been long forgotten among Churches of Christ. Even his biographers do not bring out Lipscomb's belief in an earthly millennial kingdom. Indeed, such views appear strange, irrelevant, and disturbing—if not blatantly heretical—to most people in the twentieth-century tradition.

That fact alone provides one telling indicator of the change Churches of Christ underwent in the opening decades of the twentieth century.

Selected Sources

Epigraph: Lipscomb, *Civil Government*, p. 28.

Hughes, Richard T. "The Apocalyptic Origins of the Churches of Christ and the Triumph of Modernism." *Religion and American Culture: A Journal of Interpretation* 2 (Summer 1992), 181-214. [I am indebted to this important article for the conceptual links between Stone and Lipscomb, for some of the insights into Lipscomb's theology, and for the quotes from Lambert and Wallace.]

Lipscomb, David. *Civil Government: Its Origin, Mission, and Destiny and the Christian's Relation to It.* Nashville: McQuiddy, 1889.

_____. "The Kingdom of God." *Gospel Advocate* 45 (May 21, 1903), 328.

_____. "A Monstrous Dogma." *Gospel Advocate* 23 (November 24, 1881), 740-41.

_____. "The Ruin and Redemption of the World." In *Salvation from Sin*, pp. 109-28. 1913, reprint ed., Nashville: *Gospel Advocate*, 1950.

Wallace, Foy, Jr. "The Lipscomb Theory of Civil Government." *Bible Banner* 5 (October 1943).

Chapter 13

God's Chosen Vessels

The poor of this world were the chosen vessels of mercy, the especially honored and blessed of God. They, as a class, constitute his elect.

—David Lipscomb (1869)

In June of 1873 a deadly cholera epidemic struck Nashville, Tennessee. Dozens of people began dying daily, and on one particularly dark day—Black Friday, June 20—at least 72 people died. The epidemic raged throughout the month of June, and when it was over more than a thousand people had succumbed to the disease—about one out of every forty residents of the city.

Many of those who were financially able, including many Christians, fled the city in panic to escape the threat. So many fled, in fact, that for several days trains were enlarged to accommodate the mass exodus.

The hardest hit were the poor and destitute, especially among the black population. At least 200 blacks died in the New Bethel Community in the southern part of the city. Some people who had the resources to leave the city chose to stay and work among the sick and dying. These included many

*Report in a Nashville newspaper describing the height
of the 1873 cholera epidemic.*

physicians, most preachers, and the Catholic nuns of
Nashville. They also included David Lipscomb and many
young people from among the restoration movement in
Nashville.

Though Lipscomb himself was not physically strong
at the time, he worked for days among the poor and sick,
placing his own life at risk. He helped distribute food and
supplies. He went into the homes of destitute blacks and
helped to clean and feed them. And he used his buggy to

carry the nuns—whom he deeply respected for their courage—to and from the places they were needed.

The number of Christians who had fled the city in face of the disease troubled Lipscomb. "Every individual, white or black, that dies from neglect and want of proper food and nursing," he wrote as the epidemic was nearing its end, "is a reproach to the professors of the Christian religion in the vicinity of Nashville."

Christians are people who have taken a solemn pledge, he wrote a short time later: "The pledge that we solemnly make in our profession of faith in Christ and of our baptism into him, is that we strive to reproduce his life before the world in our own lives." How would Christ have responded to the epidemic and the "wild panic" that seized so many people? Lipscomb asked. "Had he been a resident of Nashville with ten, twenty, one hundred dollars, what would he have done?" Would he have rushed off to some place of refuge and left the poor to suffer? The answer, to Lipscomb, was crystal clear: Christ would have stayed in the city and used all of his means to relieve the suffering.

This episode in Lipscomb's life, perhaps more than any other, reveals the fundamental nature of the Christian faith as he understood it. For Lipscomb true Christianity was inextricably wrapped up with regard for the poor. Indeed, his writings over nearly fifty years proclaim his deep conviction that ministry to the poor serves as a fundamental identifying mark of the true church.

The economic and political upheavals of the post-Civil War period provide the backdrop for Lipscomb's concerns. For the nation as a whole, the 1870s and 1880s were watershed years. It was an age of big business, robber barons, exploding industrialism, and powerful railroad companies. It was the age of Andrew Carnegie, John Rockefeller, Pierpont Morgan, and the "Gospel of Wealth." It was an age when some ministers assured their urban flocks that "Godliness is in league with riches."

But across the country serious tensions mounted between workers and industrialists. Labor strikes broke out in record numbers in this period (over 35,000 of them through the end of the century). In 1877 a massive railroad strike led to open violence in many cities. Working people increasingly mounted assaults on the privileges of the rich and the corrupting power of wealth. Meanwhile, throughout the South widespread economic devastation and poverty remained. For decades income levels in the South remained significantly lower than in the North.

Lipscomb himself experienced great hardship during and after the war. He said that for a time he lived "in a condition of almost actual starvation," and that he visited many families "in which we felt that every mouth full of food we ate was taken from women and children who must suffer for the want of it." He noted in 1866 that, while many Southern Christians shared the "general desolation" of the war, there were "brethren North of us who have grown rich by the very circumstances that impoverished our brethren South."

Lipscomb identified deeply with the common people and the poor, and this identification undergirded his most fundamental convictions about the church and the challenges it faced in the post-war period.

One of these fundamental convictions was that "the church is the especial legacy of God to the poor of the earth." They were the chosen vessels through which God most often had chosen to work. The Old Testament prophets were poor and "often clothed in sackcloth." Jesus was born into a poor family and lived among the "laboring, toiling classes" throughout his youth. During his ministry, Jesus lived as "a homeless wanderer on the earth" and had no where to lay his head. "He mingled with the poor in their homes, ate of their coarse barley loaves, and shared their frugal fare." And when Jesus chose his apostles, he chose them from the "working class, the fishermen, the laboring people."

Lipscomb thus concluded that the "poor of this world were the chosen vessels of mercy, the especially honored and blessed of God. They, as a class, constitute his elect." It followed, Lipscomb often repeated, that the "great mass of his true and honored followers, in all ages of the world, have been, ever must be, from the poor."

From this conviction flowed major implications for the life and work of the church. One was that, since God adapted the Christian faith to the "common people," they were the ones "best fitted to maintain and spread that religion." The common people are reached more easily with the gospel, Lipscomb thought, and "generally make the best members when converted." For without worldly wealth and greatness "to engross his care and to hold his affections," such a person more readily learns to depend on God and submit to the divine will. Such people are better able to maintain the spirit of self-denial and resist the temptation to compromise with the world.

Lipscomb believed, conversely, that wealth generally corrupted the church, and he often spoke sharply about it. "The rich, and worse, those not rich who aspire to ape and court the rich, are the greatest corrupters of the church," he wrote in a common refrain. This happens because "worldly possessions, honors, [and] responsibilities above a modest competence steal the time, wean the affections, and hinder service to God." They lead people to fall into "the habit of judging by a different standard from the Savior." When the rich embrace the faith, he said, "ninety times out of every hundred their influence is to corrupt the church, lower the standard of morality, and relax all discipline in a church."

Another implication of God's special regard for the poor and common people was that churches must seek to maintain an atmosphere where the poor will feel welcome and not alienated. Above all others they should feel at home in the church. But wealth so changes things that they "cannot conform to its customs and they do not feel at home." For this reason, Lipscomb deplored the pouring of money into church buildings. "When I hear of a church setting out to build a fine house," he wrote, "I give that church up. Its usefulness as a church of Christ is at an end."

For the same reason, Lipscomb was concerned about the effects of wealth on the work and aspirations of preachers. Their central work should be among the poor and common people, but large salaries turned their heads in another direction. "To pay large salaries," Lipscomb wrote, "is to excite the thirst for wealth" and "corrupt the simplicity of the life of the preacher. This unfits him for successful work among the common people." He wrote that preachers "who have been fed and kept by the wealthy at their homes of comfort and elegance, whose education and refinement are shocked by the ignorance, the dirt, the coarseness of the poor, and wicked, find it a severe trial to be compelled to go among them."

Furthermore, such salaries put a gag in the preacher's mouth. "The preacher will cater to his supporters," Lipscomb wrote, "hence we universally find that the sins of the rich are glossed over and apologized for, while the lesser sins of the poor are exaggerated and condemned." "Especially is this so," he added, "in fashionable and wealthy churches and communities."

Preachers should maintain a measure of independence. It is not wrong to receive help from churches, Lipscomb thought, but preachers should have a "calling or craft" to fall back upon. A preacher needs such independence so he can "snap his fingers in the face of the wealthy and fashionable who corrupt the church by demanding as the price of their support that the teacher should wink at their sins, and polish over their shortcomings."

Lipscomb charged that the "whole plan of a Preacher's

putting himself up to the highest bidder, shifting about from place to place, for the sake of a little higher salary, is at once a degradation to Christianity." "Don't seek the rich and honorable to preach to," he admonished, "but preach to the poor, the neglected, the degraded, and if you live poor, you will... be one of the world's true heroes and Heaven's crowned victors."

The cholera epidemic of 1873 provides one of the most illuminating glimpses into David Lipscomb's view of the fundamental character of the church. "Christ came to save the lost, enlighten the ignorant, to lift up the down-trodden, the offcast, the outcast," he wrote a few years after the epidemic, "and unless we have his Spirit we are none of his."

"The crowning characteristic of the Christian religion in the esteem of its founder is that the 'poor have the gospel preached to them.'" The church that failed to make this its most important work, Lipscomb was convinced, could scarcely claim to be a true church of Christ.

Selected Sources

Epigraph: Lipscomb, "Who Are to Blame?" *Gospel Advocate* 11 (May 6, 1869), 422.

Dunnavant, Anthony. "David Lipscomb on the Church and the Poor." *Restoration Quarterly* 33 (1991), 75-85. [I am indebted to this article for some of the references used in this chapter.]

Hooper, Robert. *Crying in the Wilderness: A Biography of David Lipscomb.* Nashville: David Lipscomb College, 1979.

Lipscomb, David. "Christ and the Working People." *Gospel Advocate* (June 4, 1896), 356-7.

_____. "Fine Houses for Worship." *Gospel Advocate* 39 (January 28, 1892), 52.

_____. "Preachers or Teachers, No. 2." *Gospel Advocate* 15 (June 5, 1873), 529-35.

_____. "Preaching to the Poor." *Gospel Advocate* 15 (May 29, 1873), 508-12.

Trachtenberg, Alan. *The Incorporation of America: Culture and Society in the Gilded Age*. New York: Hill and Wang, 1982.

Chapter 14

Faithful Shepherds

Controlling the church by virtue of authority of office is unknown in the Scriptures. All should seek to control simply and only through the authority of truth, impressed by lives of godliness, purity and love.

—David Lipscomb (1871)

In 1870 John D. Rockefeller incorporated the Standard Oil Company of Ohio, and within ten years his corporation controlled about 90 percent of the oil business in America. "The Standard Oil Company brooks no competition," said a congressional investigating committee in 1886; "its settled policy and firm determination is to crush out all who may be rash enough to enter the field against it."

Rockefeller's name became a symbol of a new form of business organization that emerged in America in the three decades following the Civil War: the corporation. "The system of corporate life," an observer wrote in 1869, is "a new power, for which our language contains no name." Corporate forms of ownership had emerged in the railroad companies of the 1850s and by the 1870s had become commonplace. By the end of the nineteenth century the apparatus of twentieth-century corporate life was in place.

Organization and efficiency, along with obedience and loyalty, became the chief virtues of the new corporate order. Shareholders willingly surrendered authority over their investment to a centralized body, the board of directors. Such centralized control made for greater efficiency and greater profits. As Rockefeller put it, "The day of combination is here to stay. Individualism has gone, never to return."

The incorporation of America brought sweeping changes to American society. The new corporate order not only transformed the way America did business; more profoundly, it transformed basic cultural values and the ways people thought.

As incorporation became a nationwide system, the result was a more tightly structured society with more hierarchical forms of authority and control. The new urban architecture symbolized the shift. "Even the most rationally designed skyscrapers," one historian has written, "still presented themselves as statements of implacable power."

It was inevitable that the corporate and managerial revolution that so reshaped American society would effect the American churches. We might say that Protestant denominations also followed the pattern of "incorporation." Organizational efficiency and centralized control became key concerns of the growing urban churches. As a result, denominational agencies and bureaucracies steadily proliferated.

Against these trends, David Lipscomb and the *Gospel Advocate* held up a profoundly different vision of the church. For over fifty years, Lipscomb spoke out sharply against the forms of organization and power represented by the new "corporate" model. Not only did he become a crusty foe of the missionary societies promoted in the restoration movement, he also opposed the concept of an "official" eldership.

Throughout his long editorial career, Lipscomb often

David Lipscomb with his niece: he prized simplicity and believed that worldly forms of power and organization had no place in God's scheme of things.

addressed issues and questions regarding church leadership. One of his steady themes was that elders in a congregation were not "officers" in the usual sense of that term. People typically use the term "officer," he said, as "one who is appointed to do a work, which he could not do without that appointment." Thus, a sheriff can arrest someone by the authority of his office, but a person without such official power cannot. Lipscomb was emphatic that Christ's church has no officers in this sense.

To the objection that elders and deacons are called officers in the Bible, Lipscomb replied that such a concept rests on a mistranslation of 1 Tim. 3:2 ("If any man desire the *office* of a bishop he desires a good work."). He argued that no word in the original language corresponded to the present-day concept of office, and that a literal translation would read, "If any one desire overseeing he desires a good work."

The work of elders is to instruct, admonish, encourage and strengthen the disciples, and direct in worship, Lipscomb said. "But cannot they do this as well before as after their ordination," he asked; "and is it not the duty of every Christian to have this same care one for another, and for the well-being of the church as a whole?" Elders' work is "a work in which any may engage, but which is especially assigned to certain ones on account of fitness of character and aptitude for the work."

Lipscomb made this point to underscore the nature of elders' authority. "We believe that no office in the church invests with a particle of authority," he wrote in a common statement. "Office [simply] means duty—it places upon one the obligation to do a certain work. It gives no authority or power. The elders are not to rule by official authority or power but to do it in love."

In Lipscomb's view the authority of elders did not reside in any office or appointment but was simply a moral authority rooted in character and faithfulness. "Controlling the church by virtue of authority of office is unknown in the Scriptures," he wrote. "All should seek to control simply and only through the authority of truth, impressed by lives of godliness, purity and love." On another occasion he wrote that the only authority possessed by elders lies in "the moral weight their wisdom and devotion carry with them, gained through obedience to the will of God."

Given this view of elders' authority, Lipscomb was clear about how one became an elder. It was not by election or appointment. It was not by stepping into some office. Rather it was by doing the work of an elder. One becomes an elder or deacon "just as carpenters and blacksmiths are made, by laboring, studying, practicing the things in which they are engaged."

The congregation then simply recognizes their work. It does this, not by holding an election, but by "looking out from among themselves," that is, by conferring together to see who possesses the qualifications and who is already doing the work. When the congregation agrees on who that is then "the Holy Spirit has already appointed such bishops and deacons." Formal ordination was not necessary. Indeed, Lipscomb said that he himself "had never gone through an ordination process to any office and could not even urge the brethren to have it done."

Lipscomb addressed these matters often over the years because of the abuse of authority he frequently observed in the churches. He lamented the growing "officialism" that focused on the power and honor of the position rather than on servitude.

"So far as we have observed," he wrote in 1877, " the electing and setting apart of officers has been a complete farce in the churches." He explained:

> The usual plan of appointing them is for a few of the active and influential brethren to confer among themselves, as to who carries the most weight and would make the church most respectable, with respectable people, agree among themselves, some one nominates him publicly, a few vote for him, the rest do not vote, not liking to vote publicly against a brother, they ... get two or three preachers and officers to lay their hands upon the heads of those elected, kneel down and pray, and then declare him inducted into office.

Lipscomb saw several problems with elevating the work of elders to the status of an office. Most serious was the usurping of authority that belonged only to God. Any man or set of men who attempts "to exercise authority in a church by virtue of some official appointment," he wrote, "or to assert that they have rights and authority as officers above others and assume to exert their rights, without the full approval of the members," are lording it over the flock. They are "exalting their authority at the expense of the authority of

Jesus Christ and the Holy Spirit." And when that happens, the congregation should resist, "even to the disruption of the body."

A church's decisions should be the decisions of the church as a whole, Lipscomb thought, not "arbitrary rulings" based on the elder's authority. Elders should "voice the judgment of the church. They can do this only by consulting all." This means that they must consider the "complaints and desires of the humblest member."

Another problem with "officialism," Lipscomb thought, was that it eroded individual responsibility for the church's work. The work of the church rests upon all the members, according to the gifts God has given. The overseers encourage, guide, and admonish each person to develop that gift and grow in that work. They take the lead in good works and persuade by their own example.

But the "official board of elders and deacons" creates different expectations. People tend to assume that such officers have a special authority—that they are assigned work that no one else can do. So the members elect their officers, then assume that "it is the officers' duty to look after the church interests and the members can rest at ease."

According to William Lipscomb, David's brother, such an unscriptural system tends to regard Christians as "fledglings with mouths agape ready to receive dainty morsels provided and prepared by human manipulation." It views them as "timid lambs" needing "watch-dog protection." Christians certainly need encouragement and exhortation from wise old Christians, he added, but not the control of "the so-called eldership."

E. G. Sewell, Lipscomb's long-time editorial associate, fully shared the Lipscombs' strictures against "officialism." After surveying each use of the term "elder" in the New Testament, he insisted that the term referred to nothing more than age. It was never used as an official term, but referred only to the "senior members" in a congregation. He even argued that the "elder women" in 1 Tim. 5:2 "are just as much officers as the older men are." Neither were actually "officers" in the church, he concluded; rather, both made up the "senior members" who led the congregation by their example and teaching.

David Lipscomb and his circle of editorial colleagues stood firmly against the tide of "incorporation" that swept America and American churches in the late nineteenth century. Worldly forms of power and authority, however efficient and cost effective they might prove, had no place in God's scheme of things.

God's kingdom, they felt, stood in sharp contrast to all the kingdoms and institutions of this world. God was creating a new order, and one day God would establish that new order over all the earth. In the meantime, Lipscomb thought, God sought wise and willing workers, not elected officers, to lead the way.

Selected Sources

Epigraph: Lipscomb, "Church Work," *Gospel Advocate* 13 (August 31, 1871), 795.

Chandler, Alfred D. *The Visible Hand: The Managerial Revolution in American Business.* Cambridge: Harvard University, 1977.

Lipscomb, David. "Church Authority." *Gospel Advocate* 19 (April 12, 1877), 232.

_____. "Officers and Officialism in the Church of God." *Gospel Advocate* 9 (July 18, 1867), 567-68.

_____. "Work of Elders." *Gospel Advocate* 43 (August 15, 1901), 521.

_____, and E. G. Sewell. *Questions Answered*. Ed. M. C. Kurfees. Nashville: Gospel Advocate, 1921.

Sewell, E. G. "Elders." *Gospel Advocate* 14 (September 5, 1872), 829-34.

Trachtenberg, Alan. *The Incorporation of America: Culture and Society in the Gilded Age*. New York: Hill and Wang, 1982.

Chapter 15

The Trouble with Stained Glass

The Lord is not attracted by imposing temples,
worldly show, nor fine entertainments.

—Benjamin Franklin (1872)

"A mighty torrent of worldliness [is] now perverting and corrupting the pure and holy worship prescribed and authorized by our Lord Jesus Christ," wrote Benjamin Franklin in February of 1872. "This worldly and carnal display will send grief home to many hearts of the old saints. Many thousands now living will grieve."

When he wrote these words, Franklin (1812-1878) was the editor of the *American Christian Review* in Cincinnati, Ohio, a weekly magazine that during the 1860s and 70s was the most influential periodical in the restoration movement. He also stood among the most prominent evangelists and debaters in the second generation of the movement.

What so aroused Franklin's deep concern in February of 1872? What was this "worldly and carnal display" he spoke of?

Just across town, the Central Christian Church had just completed its new building that month and held the dedication service. The building was a grand and impressive structure. Its cost was also impressive—upwards of $125,000 (at a time when the average total wealth of adult males in the U.S. was under $2,400). It contained elaborate furnishings, a Catherine wheel window (a round stained glass window named after a fourth-century Christian martyr), and an $8,000 dollar pipe organ.

Franklin and many others in the movement found this lavish building deeply offensive. They viewed it as a symbol of a disturbing trend—the move toward big-city respectability and the desire to accommodate the growing urban affluence.

The backdrop for these tensions was the dramatic growth of American cities in the two decades after the Civil War. These were the years when cities were "springing up and growing great and splendid as it were in a night." Streams of people moved from farms and rural areas to the new commercial centers. Whole towns sometimes disappeared, and farmland in some cases was left to revert to woodland. One minister observed with alarm in 1874 that "the country is now but a suburb of the city," its "simple manners, moderate desires, and autonomous life … as good as disappeared."

As the cities grew so did the affluence and power of the churchgoing middle-class. The blessings and responsibilities of wealth, not surprisingly, became a common theme in Protestant preaching in the late 1860s and throughout the 70s. One person wrote in this period that preachers should not "inveigh against luxuries, for the sum of wealth cannot be too great, if well used, and luxuries are the only foundation of large wealth in any community." A writer in the *Christian Standard* declared that "No one need be afraid of earning too much money. It is a sin against God to do so, if he gives us the opportunity."

The skyline of Cincinnati, Ohio, in 1859: "congregations vied with one another to possess the tallest steeple as a symbol of wealth and prestige."

As middle-class churchgoing people prospered and their number grew in the cities, they built church buildings that reflected their prosperity. In this period, one historian wrote, "costly and imposing edifices were being built to match the increasing prosperity of the clientele, and congregations vied with one another to possess the tallest steeple as a symbol of wealth and prestige." Along with impressive new buildings went other upgraded features: expensive pipe organs, professional musicians, and more refined, eloquent, and educated preachers.

The evangelistic success of these new affluent urban churches was primarily among middle-class, white-collar workers who had come to the city from rural areas, not among the poor, the destitute, and the day-laborers whose ranks were also swelling. The poor and laboring people remained, on the whole, largely untouched—and often unseen—by the urban churches.

Protestant church leaders in general found little to criticize in the prevailing economic and social conditions of the age. For the most part, they were unrestrained in their support of *laissez faire* capitalism and sharply opposed to the rise of organized labor unions. "In 1876," as Henry May put it, "Protestantism presented a massive, almost unbroken front in its defense of the social status quo."

As the churches of the restoration movement grew in the new cities, they followed the same trends. Leaders expressed the need to improve the church's image and to tap into the wealth in the cities and use it for Christian purposes. Some talked about the need to get beyond the old rural, small town ways and attitudes, and become more like the successful city churches.

Though city church leaders talked about reaching the poor urban masses, the new buildings they erected and the refinements they employed actually served to attract respectable churchgoing people and deepen their estrangement from the poor. But few middle-class church leaders of the time saw the disparity. As one historian observed, "Very few perceived that the goals of attracting the middle-class and reaching the poor were antagonistic ones."

Isaac Errett, editor of the *Christian Standard* in Cincinnati, illustrates some of the tensions surrounding this issue. In the 1860s Errett had written strongly against expensive buildings and what they represented. "Costly edifices of worship, costly decorations, costly dress, and costly equipage are all inimical to the humility and simplicity of the religion of Jesus," he had written in 1866. "The mission of the church is preeminently to the poor. The wealthy in the church should never forget it." The church requires the wealthy "to enter her walls in plain attire, and be 'one in Christ Jesus,' with the poor and lowly." "As wealth increases, and the church grows in popular favor," he warned, "the tinsel, and glitter, and gaudiness of a carnal world [replaces] the humility, and simplicity, and affection of a spiritual church."

The Central Christian Church building in Cincinnati, completed in 1872 (shown here many years later).

But within a few years Errett was sounding a some-what different note. In 1868 the church in New Castle, Pennsylvania called upon him to deliver the dedication sermon for its new $90,000 building. (It happened to be the home church of the wealthy Phillips family that financed Errett's magazine.) The local newspaper described the new building as built in "Florid Gothic Early English Style," and gave special praise to the stained glass windows (with their "richly colored borders and heads"). Errett later defended the building against detractors who thought it too lavish. Despite some objectionable features, he wrote, "pride did not prompt it" but rather "the money has been laid out for perma-nency rather than for show."

In 1872 Errett also vigorously defended the new Central building against Benjamin Franklin's censures. The congregational leaders, he insisted, were not vain and proud men but rather "whole-hearted, humble, earnest men" engaged in a "noble enterprise." Furthermore, he explained, the construction of so large a building required that it "be more or less ornamental to save it from being ungainly and offensive to good taste." And finally, he assured people that such a building would attract the poor, not repel them. "Poor Catholics are not unwilling to go to the most splendid cathe-drals," he concluded, "and poor Jews are perfectly at home in their most costly temples."

Benjamin Franklin and his associate editor John F. Rowe viewed the situation very differently. They charged flatly that the Central church leaders were "aping" the denom-inations in the quest for urban respectability. The leaders were determined, Franklin said, "to make the church a fash-ionable place of resort and entertainment."

> We would blush to talk of the "ancient order," the "gospel restored," returning to the "primitive order," the "Man of sorrows," who "had not where to lay his head"—and teaching, "Be not conformed to this world, but be you transformed," "Love not the world nor the things of the world," in this temple of folly and pride.

Franklin quoted from the newspaper's description of the building: "The fine effect of light, warmed and tinted as it passes through the stained windows, will strike every beholder the moment he enters the auditorium. It is the dim religious tone, so admirably adapted to a place of worship." In response, Franklin asked: what about "the thousands of poor saints that cannot have even a house in which to meet, to say nothing of the 'dim religious tone' to impart a worshipful feeling?"

Franklin pressed the question. Will the poor find "this house of fashion and splendor" the place for them? They will not, he answered, "nor will the Lord, who requires the poor to have the gospel preached to them, go there," for the Lord is "not attracted by imposing temples, worldly show, nor fine entertainments." This last phrase was probably an allusion to the "grand Organ Concert" sponsored by the Central Church shortly after the dedication.

John F. Rowe, Franklin's associate editor, followed up with an article entitled "How to Drive Away the Poor." He laid down an axiom: "there must be a correspondence between the gorgeousness of the edifice and those who take possession of it." And so it follows, he reasoned, that "if you build a temple of fashion, you must expect the fashionable ones to make their grand Sunday rendezvous." A building may be built ostensibly to serve the poor but with time "a certain class of the aristocracy" will possess it and set the social standards. The poor person will "soon see where he belongs."

The fact is, Rowe said, that "Churches compete in

architecture just as ladies compete in the fashions." A few churches build great buildings, and other churches grow dissatisfied with their lot. So they start a building program, and mount "a great ado about getting money." There is much "wrangling and jangling of the building committee." At long last they complete their impressive building and stage a "grand consummation." Three months later, however, "the pastor looks around to pay his compliments to the poor, but the poor have escaped to the lanes, the by-ways and the hedges."

Franklin and Rowe in Ohio, like David Lipscomb in Tennessee (see Chapter 13), believed that the building of great church buildings basically grew out of "carnal pride." Such buildings, they thought, both reflected and helped create an ethos that worked against the lowly spirit of Jesus and the gospel.

For many people in the restoration movement of the late nineteenth century, that was precisely the trouble with stained glass.

Selected Sources

Epigraph: Franklin, "Central Christian Church." *American Christian Review* 15 (February 20, 1872), 60.

Boggs, John. "Money." *Christian Standard* 8 (August 27, 1873), 265.

Errett, Isaac. "Conformity to the World." *Christian Standard* 4 (July 24, 1869), 236.

_____. "Is It Pride and Carnality?" *Christian Standard* 7 (March 2, 1872), 68.

_____. "Social Development." *Christian Standard* 1 (August 4, 1866), 140.

Franklin, Benjamin. "Central Christian Church." *American Christian Review* 15 (March 26, 1872), 100.

Harrell, David E., Jr. *The Social Sources of Division in the Disciples of Christ, 1865-1900*. Atlanta: Publishing Systems, 1973.

May, Henry F. *Protestant Churches and Industrial America*. New York: Harper & Brothers, 1949.

Rowe, John F. "How to Drive Away the Poor." *American Christian Review* 15 (March 12, 1872), 84-5.

Willis, Wendell Lee. "A Sociological Study of Tensions in the Restoration Movement in the North, 1866-1878." M.A. Thesis, Abilene Christian University, 1973.

Chapter 16

The Blessing of Tradition

The tradition of the Church has value... not because it comes through an infallible channel, but because it exhibits a consensus of intelligent interpretation.

—B. A. Hinsdale (1879)

I n 1831 and 1832 the Frenchman Alexis de Tocqueville traveled for nine months in America observing the nation's life and assessing its distinctive character. His observations remain some of the most trenchant ever written about the young American nation.

What particularly struck Tocqueville was the sense of rootlessness and the disregard for tradition that he observed. For Americans, he wrote, "there are no traditions, or common habits, to forge links between their minds."

This loss of binding traditions was enhanced by the newness of the American land and by the social mobility of those who tamed and settled it. With the West opening up, Tocqueville said, people "arrive in the depth of the wilderness without knowing one another. There is nothing of tradition, family feeling, or example to restrain them." In general, he concluded, "nobody's position is quite stable. The woof of time is broken and the track of past generations lost."

What was true of the social life of early nineteenth-century Americans was also true of their religious life. People not only veered from one place to another in their quest for new land, but also from one church to another in the quest for a new, more meaningful faith. The result was profound religious change and unrest. Indeed, as Nathan Hatch put it, the "first third of the nineteenth century experienced a period of religious ferment, chaos, and originality unmatched in American history."

In this period of intense ferment, religious traditions took a beating. People increasingly challenged traditional religious authorities. The Christian tradition, in the eyes of many people, became little more than a sordid tale of corruption and oppression, a story of "priestcraft" and its enslavement of people's minds. The old time-worn traditions, after all, were maintained by clerics, creeds, and hierarchical church structures.

To a people estranged from the past and living in a seemingly pristine and undefiled land, only one option seemed to make sense: to dismiss tradition entirely and start fresh—right from the beginning.

The growing Protestant churches of this period, whether Baptist, Methodist, or "Christian," attempted to do just that. They distanced themselves from both Catholic and Protestant traditions, and called for the restoration of primitive Christianity. "No creed but the Bible" became the common rallying cry (see Chapter 3).

The confidence that one could indeed break free of the past was rooted in the American Revolution. The young American nation, most people believed, was the scene of momentous events—a "new order of the ages" raised up by God. The American Revolution had done nothing less than usher in a new epoch in human history. And in this new epoch the old oppressive order had been defeated, its tired and unworkable political traditions cast off.

Alexander Campbell fully shared such convictions. The remaining challenge, he thought, was to extend the same revolution from the political realm to the religious—to cast off tired and oppressive Christian traditions and to usher in a new epoch of "gospel-liberty."

Campbell described how, after coming to America in 1809, he entered a period of profound rethinking in which he attempted to make a complete break with all theological tradition. He said he struggled to read the Bible as if he had never read it before. That task was "arduous beyond expression," he admitted, for he had to unlearn most of what he had been taught about Protestant theology. In the process he rejected the Westminster Confession—large portions of which he had memorized as a child—for it was, he said, little more than "trash" which theologians had "interlarded" with scripture.

So successful were his efforts to break with tradition, he claimed, that after 1812 his mind was "for a time, set loose from all its former moorings." In this state, he concluded, "I was placed on a new eminence—a new peak of the mountain of God, from which the whole landscape of Christianity presented itself to my mind in a new attitude and position." Only from this vantage point, he said, was he able at last to rediscover and restore the "ancient gospel and order of things."

Out of this experience Campbell laid down a basic principle: one can read the Bible properly and rise above sectarian strife only by approaching scripture "without a single inclination to any opinion, theory, or system whatever." Though admittedly a difficult task, one must strive to read "the Bible as if it had dropped from heaven into his hands alone."

For Campbell this meant that one could jettison as unnecessary the whole library of creeds, confessions, homilies, and commentaries spanning fifteen centuries. For all of this contained nothing that was not more plainly and precisely taught in scripture. Indeed, "on the subject of religion," Campbell could write in one of his more iconoclastic moods, "I am fully persuaded that nothing but the inspired scriptures ought ever to have been published."

This attitude toward the Christian tradition, it should be noted, was not a simple ignorance of the past or an untutored scorn of it. Considerable erudition, historical breadth, and intellectual sophistication marked Campbell's thought. He knew the broad outlines of the Christian tradition fairly well, especially the Protestant Reformation, often citing its creeds and confessions in his polemics. He appreciated Martin Luther and other earlier reformers for their efforts at protest and recovery. Furthermore, Campbell did not reject all historic creeds out of hand, but rather their use as tests of fellowship.

Still, the predominant note was strongly negative. "The leprosy of apostasy has spread over all Christendom, Catholic and Protestant," he wrote in a characteristic statement; as a result, "the Christian religion has been for ages interred in the rubbish of human invention and tradition." What Christianity needed most, Campbell thought, was a clean break with tradition. And he was supremely confident that his own "reformation" movement had done just that. Indeed, a fundamental premise was the bold claim that "We brought no [traditional] doctrines with us at all into the…proposed Reformation."

This attitude toward tradition remained characteristic of Campbell's restoration movement throughout the nineteenth century and into the twentieth. Indeed, it characterized much American Protestantism in the period. The first half of the nineteenth century, as one historian has noted, was a time when tradition "suffered the perverse fortune of having

*Burke Aaron Hinsdale (1837–1900): one of the first in the restoration
movement to emphasize the positive value of tradition.*

only the case against it presented fully and explicitly."

In 1879, however, one man sounded a new note in the
movement. That year Burke A. Hinsdale (1837-1900), a
preacher and president of Hiram College in Ohio, published
a book entitled, *Ecclesiastical Tradition: Its Origin and Early
Growth; Its Place in the Churches, and Its Value.* Here Hinsdale
suggested that, though tradition easily weighs down and
distorts the faith, it could also serve an important clarifying
and stabilizing function. In explicitly recognizing and under-

scoring this positive function of tradition Hinsdale stood virtually alone in the movement.

Hinsdale had graduated from Hiram College in 1860, then preached for several years in Ohio. From 1864 to 1869 he served as associate editor for the *Christian Standard*, then in 1869 became professor of philosophy, English, and political science at Hiram. He was an intimate and lifelong friend of James A. Garfield (who was also a Hiram graduate), and after Garfield's assassination in 1881 wrote a biography of him and edited his papers.

Throughout much of his 1879 work on tradition, Hinsdale sounded familiar notes. He upheld the Protestant ideal of "scripture alone" against the Roman Catholic claim to an infallible church tradition. He also argued, as had Campbell before him, that "Protestants have never really understood Protestantism." For they rejected the authority of tradition in principle but clung to many extra-biblical traditions in practice. Infant baptism, sprinkling, diocesan bishops, creeds as tests of fellowship—all of these, Hinsdale argued, were merely traditional practices for which Protestants sought biblical support. They had found such support, he insisted, only by means of "unnatural interpretation" and "far-fetched inferences."

The most serious inconsistency of Protestantism was its use of creeds as tests of fellowship. "No other error that the Reformers fell into," Hinsdale wrote, "has so retarded the restoration of primitive Christianity." Neither the Protestants nor the Catholics, he said, have trusted individuals alone with the Bible: the Catholic binds people to the church, the Protestant binds them to creeds. Protestantism, as a result, quickly developed its own powerful, inviolable traditions.

These arguments were all familiar ones in the restoration movement. What was new in Hinsdale's book was the recognition (1) that the movement itself had laid down its own venerated tradition and (2) that tradition, despite its pitfalls, served an important conserving function.

On the first point, Hinsdale pointed out that "No Christian body can ever be found that has reached the age of half a century, which has not something that answers for a tradition." One may begin with a scorn of tradition and a desire to break completely with it, but one quickly and inevitably creates a new tradition, one carrying its own considerable weight and authority.

The restoration movement, Hinsdale observed, had developed such a tradition, though few people were able to see or admit it. "We too have developed our *corpus traditorum* held in a kind of semi-sacred awe, and appealed to as of the fathers." People therefore could argue that "Such and such has been the uniform teaching among us," and feel that they were advancing an argument of some weight.

Hinsdale thought that people needed to acknowledge the fact of tradition and then face up to it. "We cannot cut loose from the past," he wrote; "we must respect the historical development of doctrines, institutions, and societies." Denying this meant saying in effect that "both the individual man and the human race must begin its mental existence anew every day."

Tradition exercises a vital stabilizing function. It "aids in securing a continuity of intellectual, moral, and religious life from age to age. It furnishes a large share of that mental inertia without which spiritual stability is impossible."

Furthermore, tradition helps one discern the great central doctrines of the faith. "The tradition of the Church has value," Hinsdale insisted, "not because it comes through an infallible channel, but because it exhibits a consensus of intelligent interpretation." Despite the "fearful apostasies" across the centuries, "the great body of the Historic Church has preserved the central facts, commands, and promises of the Gospel."

At the same time, however, tradition easily gets too

firm a hold on one. Hinsdale recognized that it easily "makes the present the slave of the past, and forever confines a man to the mental circle in which his father walked."

Hinsdale best summarized his view of tradition in these words: "Called infallible...tradition is a deadly thing; looked upon as human but constantly deferred to and venerated ... it is a barrier to progress; respected but thoroughly discussed and calmly weighed, it is a source both of beauty and of strength."

In contrast to Alexander Campbell and many others of his time, Burke Hinsdale believed that the human mind cannot be "set loose from all its former moorings." He insisted rather that "the past ever casts its light and shade over the present and the future."

Recognizing that fact, he thought, demanded great wariness, to be sure, but it also gave cause for considerable thanksgiving.

Selected Sources

Epigraph: Hinsdale, *Ecclesiastical Tradition*, p. 170.

Campbell, Alexander. "Anecdotes, Incidents and Facts, Connected with the Origin and Progress of the Current Reformation." *Millennial Harbinger* 3rd series 5 (June 1848), 344-5.

_____. "Christendom in its Dotage." *Millennial Harbinger* 5 (August 1834), 372ff.

Hatch, Nathan O. *The Democratization of American Christianity*. New Haven: Yale University, 1989.

Hinsdale, B. A. *Ecclesiastical Tradition: Its Origin and Early Growth; Its Place in the Churches, and Its Value*. Cincinnati: Standard Publishing, 1879.

_____. "The Roman Catholic and Protestant Habits of Mind." *Christian Standard* 16 (November 5, 1881), 353.

_____. "Written Creeds and Doctrinal Uniformity." *Christian Standard* 6 (March 25, 1871), 89.

Hughes, Richard T., and C. Leonard Allen. *Illusions of Innocence: Protestant Primitivism in America, 1630-1875*. Chicago: University of Chicago, 1988.

Morrow, Ralph. "The Great Revival, the West, and the Crisis of the Church." In *The Frontier Re-examined*. Ed. John F. McDermott. Urbana: University of Illinois, 1967.

Chapter 17

The New Woman

*A learned Christian woman may expound the
scriptures and urge obedience to them, to one
hundred men and women at one time, as well as
to one hundred, one at a time, ... and no more
violate a scriptural command in one instance
than the other.*

—Silena Holman (1888)

***

"Shall the sisters pray and speak in public?"
Throughout 1888 and for several years that
followed, that question was one of the most
pressing among Churches of Christ. It aroused controversy
and debate across the pages of the *Gospel Advocate* and other
periodicals.

In March of 1888 a man wrote to David Lipscomb,
editor of the *Advocate,* suggesting that the command, "Let
your women keep silence in the churches" (1 Cor. 14:34),
prohibited women even from teaching children in the Sunday
school. Lipscomb responded that they could teach children
and even their husbands but only in a "modest deferential

manner," not in "an assuming, authoritative way." And certainly, he added, women must never stand "before promiscuous [or mixed] assemblies" but rather teach only in private.

Silena Moore Holman (1850-1915), an elder's wife from Fayetteville, Tennessee, and mother of eight children, responded to Lipscomb and the question of woman's place. She boldly challenged some of the traditional assumptions, provoking sharp and lively exchanges with Lipscomb that continued on and off for many years.

In an article entitled "Let Your Women Keep Silence," published in August 1888, Holman admitted that there would be little doubt about Paul's view of women in the church if all we had was his injunction in 1 Cor. 14:34-35. But there are other passages indicating that women were prominent workers in the early church, "and others still, *seeming* to teach differently from 1 Cor. 14:34." It is these passages, she said, that raise doubts about the traditional view of Paul's meaning.

In several lengthy articles she examined these passages, underscoring the active and public ministries of women like Deborah the judge of Israel (Judges 4-6), Anna the prophetess (Lk. 2:37-38), Priscilla who taught Apollos (Acts 18:26), the women assembled with the apostles on Pentecost (Acts 2), and Phillip's four daughter's who prophesied (Acts 2:8-9). All of these provided biblical examples, she thought, of a public role for women that did not "usurp authority" over men.

She made clear her agreement with Lipscomb on one thing: "the man is the head of the woman, and should take the lead, most especially in the family relation." But she strongly disagreed that women were thereby completely removed from public leadership roles and confined entirely to the private and domestic sphere. The home was a woman's primary focus, she agreed, and public activity should never displace that; but women who possessed the God-given gifts should be allowed "to go out in the world and tell of the

Silena Moore Holman (1850–1915): outspoken advocate of the "new woman."

unsearchable riches of the gospel" and to combat the social evils that threatened the home.

Holman in fact rejected the distinction between private and public spheres that Lipscomb and most others sought to maintain. A woman could teach a man privately, they insisted, but not publicly, in her parlor but not in the assembly. Such a distinction, she argued, was much more cultural than scriptural. "Suppose a dozen men and women were in my parlor and I talked to them of the gospel and exhorted them to obey it? Exactly how many would have to be added to the number," she asked, "to make my talk and exhortation a public instead of a private one?"

She made her own answer to that question very clear. "I believe that a learned Christian woman may expound the scriptures and urge obedience to them," she stated, "to one hundred men and women at one time, as well as to one hundred, one at a time, and do much good, and no more violate a scriptural command in one instance than the other."

In numerous articles, Holman developed her views with considerable skill and verve. She dealt extensively with biblical passages, and often affirmed her commitment to biblical authority. Lipscomb's responses were usually sharp, sometimes patronizing, and occasionally marked by exasperation. Her responses to him—and to other male critics— were firm, carefully reasoned, and respectful.

Lipscomb's basic response was that God assigned woman to the domestic sphere, and when she oversteps that realm she rebels against God and threatens the stability of society. By nature and temperament, Lipscomb believed, woman was suited to this realm and no other. God had made her more emotional and less rational than man. As a result, she was wonderfully suited for nurturing children but not for public teaching or leadership.

Eve's attempt to instruct Adam in the Garden of Eden provided proof. In that story, Lipscomb asserted, the Holy Spirit was saying, "I suffered you to take the lead once; your strong emotional nature led you to violate God's word and to shipwreck a world, I cannot again trust you to lead."

God gave woman "heart-power" to fit her for being a wife and mother. But this very trait unfit her for leadership in society and church, Lipscomb stated, for it tends to "blind her to facts, shut out reason and lead her headlong where her emotions prompt her."

Silena Holman's own writings, Lipscomb charged, provided a case in point. "When she wants a thing so, her strong emotional nature and intense love will see and have it that way any how." She can no more see the plain teaching of scripture regarding woman's place than "mother Eve could see death in the goodly fruit that pleased her." In this way, Lipscomb concluded, Holman "thoroughly vindicates her womanly nature," offering living proof why God forbids women to teach and lead in the church.

In his exchanges with Holman, Lipscomb revealed clearly his deep allegiance to what historians of the period have called the "cult of true womanhood" or the "cult of domesticity." This vision of the ideal woman emerged in America between 1820 and 1860 and remained dominant until near the end of the century.

As America became industrialized, fathers steadily left the home or the farm for the workplace. With men newly caught up in careers, women were left with the chief responsibility for maintaining the home and providing spiritual and moral training for the children. As a result, the roles of wife, mother, and homemaker were heightened and idealized, and the model of "true womanhood" emerged.

This ideal permeated the women's magazines, popular books, and religious literature of the period. Four attributes stood out: purity, piety, submissiveness, and domesticity. With their superior moral purity and spiritual sensibilities, women were to restrain the natural lust and aggressiveness of husbands and sons. They were to make their homes havens of stability and nurture.

At the same time, the ideal woman was passive, dependent, deferential, and childlike. As one Christian woman put it in 1870, "God has so made the sexes that women, like children, cling to men; lean upon them as though they were superior in mind and body." Women could exert an enormous leavening, uplifting, and nurturing influence, but only by remaining properly submissive. Indeed, by remaining strictly within their ordained sphere, women served as the backbone of society.

David Lipscomb and many other leaders of the restoration movement in the 1880s held this ideal of "true womanhood" without question. It deeply shaped their interpretation of biblical teaching about the role of women.

On this basis, for example, Lipscomb, his co-editor Sewell, and most other leaders condemned the "strong-minded women" who sought the right to vote. Women voting, Sewell wrote, was based on "a principle which, if allowed to spread, threatens to destroy the most sacred of all institutions, and make America a homeless nation." Women who sought the vote, he warned, would "break the 'bond of subjection' divinely laid upon them and assert their independence; vote, hold office, electioneer, and, if necessary, fight their way to the ballot box."

By stepping beyond their divinely ordained sphere, women threatened the whole moral order of things. When women entered the public sphere, Lipscomb proclaimed, chaos resulted—"loose marriage, easy divorce, indisposition to bear children, and... attendant social impurity."

Silena Holman also assumed the cultural ideal of "true womanhood" in certain ways but begged to differ with Lipscomb at major points. Against Lipscomb, she denied that women were unfit for leadership due to their emotional nature. "The Bible nowhere intimates," she retorted, "that the mind of woman is inferior to that of man (and it is the mind that makes the leader)." Indeed, in the fields of science, the arts, education, literature, journalism, business, and the professions, "woman has come to the front and proven her ability to cope with man, in anything she may undertake."

Further, when Lipscomb charged that much of the moral disarray of American society was to be laid at the feet of women who neglected their domestic duties and sought public roles, Holman took sharp exception. "My dear sister," Lipscomb had written, "man is what his mother makes him. The great and good men are always conceded to be the work of their mothers. The bad men [too] are just as much the work of their hands."

Preposterous, replied Holman; women do not possess all the goodness in the world, and neither should they "shoulder the responsibility for all the bad." Man is the head of the woman, she argued, and he has an obligation to keep her on the right path. When she fails in her duty, he cannot excuse himself by blaming her.

With such critique, Silena Holman stood among those who in the 1890s promoted the ideal of what they called the "new woman." Proponents of the "new woman" accepted neither the passivity of the "true woman" nor the militancy of the emerging "women's rights" movement. They supported women's suffrage, women's reform societies (like the Women's Christian Temperance Union), higher education for women, and a more public role for women in the churches. They stressed loyalty to home and family and did not reject male headship. They did not promote a feminist rejection of the domestic sphere, but rather believed that more opportunities for women would make better wives and mothers.

In 1895 the *Gospel Advocate* printed an attack on the "new woman." Six months later Holman published a spirited reply. "The days of the 'clinging vine woman' are gone forever," she proclaimed. In her place a "husband will find walking by his side the bright, wide-awake companion, ... a helpmeet in the best possible sense of the term."

The "new woman" is well educated, and her education has not "impaired her feminine grace or lovable qualities in the slightest degree." She will probably marry, but will not have to "marry for a living." She knows the world around her and takes an active part in it. And she will vote when that right is granted her (only three states gave full suffrage to women at the time). "When the 'new woman'... comes into her kingdom, wide-awake, alert, thoughtful, and up to date," Holman wrote, "she will not depreciate, but... magnify and glorify the profession of motherhood."

David Lipscomb and the *Advocate* remained a staunch foe of this "new woman." She was a "usurper" of male prerogatives and dangerous to society he said in 1897. As for Silena Holman, he wrote: "It gives a body the blues to read Sister Holman's article[s]."

Holman herself modeled the "new woman" in many ways. Besides raising eight children, she worked faithfully in her church, wrote many articles for publication, and served for fifteen years as president of the Tennessee Women's Christian Temperance Union. Under her dynamic leadership the membership of that organization grew from less than 200 to over 4,000.

In 1913, two years before her death, she was still addressing "The Woman Question" in the *Gospel Advocate,* still arguing for a woman's rights to teach publicly before "mixed audiences." "Men may change with the changing conditions of modern life," she wrote; "but when women find themselves trying to keep step with their fathers, brothers, and husbands in the new order of things, the brethren stand in front of them with a drawn sword and demand a halt, because, they say, the Bible forbids, when it does nothing of the kind."

When she died in 1915, well-known evangelist T. B. Larimore preached her funeral. She had requested Larimore, she said, because "I want no man to apologize for my work, and I know he will never do that." Larimore didn't apologize. He praised her "honorable and industrious life," mentioning both her devotion to her family and her "wonderful intelligence" as a public leader.

"In her last conversation with me," Larimore concluded, "she spoke of men who had been bitter foes of her work, speaking not unkindly, but in the spirit of charity, and I want to commend that spirit to all who are here."

Two years later a portrait of Silena Holman was hung

in the Tennessee State Capitol. It was only the second time a woman had been granted that honor.

Selected Sources

Epigraph: Silena Holman, "Woman's Scriptural Status Again." *Gospel Advocate* 30 (November 21, 1888), 8.

Bailey, Fred. "Disciple Images of Victorian Womanhood." *Discipliana* 40 (Spring 1980), 7-12.

"Brother Larimore's Tribute to Mrs. Silena Moore Holman." *Gospel Advocate* 57 (October 14, 1915), 1027-28.

Holman, Silena. "Let Your Women Keep Silent." *Gospel Advocate* 30 (August 1, 1888), 8.

_____. "The Scriptural Status of Women." *Gospel Advocate* 30 (October 10, 1888), 2-3.

_____. "The 'New Woman.'" *Gospel Advocate* 28 (July 9, 1896), 438.

_____. "The New Woman, No. 2." *Gospel Advocate* 28 (July 16, 1896), 452-53.

Lipscomb, David. "Woman's Station and Work." *Gospel Advocate* 30 (October 10, 1888), 6-7.

_____. "Woman's Work in the Church." *Gospel Advocate* 30 (March 14, 1888), 6-7.

Rothman, Sheila M. *Woman's Proper Place: A History of Changing Ideals and Practices, 1870 to the Present.* New York: Basic Books, 1978.

Sewell, E. G. "Woman and Politics." *Gospel Advocate* 26 (October 22, 1884), 674.

Welter, Barbara. "The Cult of True Womanhood, 1820-1860."
    American Quarterly (1966), 151-74.

Chapter 18

Phoebe's Place

Phebe was a deaconess in the official sense of that word....whenever the necessities of the churches are such as to demand it, the order of the deaconesses should be reestablished.

—Moses E. Lard

From its early days the restoration movement of Alexander Campbell was deeply concerned with church order. From about the mid-1820s Campbell and his colleagues claimed to have restored the "ancient gospel" and its essential corollary, the "ancient order of things." Upon this original foundation, Campbell insisted, all believers could unite.

An important part of this "ancient order," Campbell stressed, was a plurality of elders and deacons in each congregation. And included among the deacons were "female deacons." In 1827 Campbell wrote that early Christians in Jerusalem "appointed female deacons, or deaconesses, to visit and wait upon the sisters. Of this sort was Phebe of Cenchrea, and other persons mentioned in the New Testament, who labored in the Gospel." From Romans 16:1

and 1 Timothy 3:11, he wrote in 1835, "it appears that females were constituted deaconesses in the primitive church. Duties to females, as well as to males, demand this." Since these specially appointed women comprised part of the church's "ancient order," it followed that they should have a place in the restored church.

Campbell apparently did not crusade for the appointment of deaconesses, but his views had considerable impact. After his two visits to the Baltimore church in 1833, for example, one of the church leaders reported that the congregation numbered sixty members and "was set in order with three Elders, three Deacons, and three Deaconesses." The nearby Chestnut Grove Church of Christ in Kelton, Pennsylvania, probably influenced by the Baltimore church, appointed two deaconesses in 1845 and two more in 1846. Some of the other congregations followed suit.

In the first several decades of the movement the appointment of deaconesses apparently was not widespread. Many prominent leaders favored it, however. Tolbert Fanning, founding editor of the *Gospel Advocate*, was one of them. "The Sisters, beyond all question, were as legitimately deacons as the brethren," he wrote. "Paul said, 'I commend to you Phoebe, our sister, who is a deacon/servant of the church at Cenchrea.' The Apostle, not only recommended the brethren at Rome to receive her as a deacon of her church, but to 'assist her in whatsoever business she had need of them.'" The name "deacon," he added, comes from the service performed: "Philip was called 'the Evangelist' because of his labor, and Phoebe was called Deacon in consequence of her labor in the cause of Christ."

Another leader who supported deaconesses was W. K. Pendleton, Campbell's editorial associate and son-in-law. In 1848 Pendleton wrote that it was "generally regarded, among our brethren, as an essential element in the restoration of primitive order, to ordain, in every church, both deacons and deaconesses." In 1870 he said: "Besides deacons, every church should have deaconesses, whose duty it is to perform such offices as cannot be so well performed by deacons, and especially such to females, as could not with delicacy and propriety be laid upon the deacons."

Robert Milligan, author of the influential book *The Scheme of Redemption*, reached a similar conclusion. "The Diaconate of the primitive Church was not confined to male members," he wrote in 1868. "Deaconesses were also appointed to attend to the wants of the sick and needy, especially of their own sex." Since the poor and needy will always remain, churches will always "require the attention of both Deacons and Deaconesses just as much as they did in the Churches of Jerusalem, Cenchrea, and Ephesus." Milligan concluded that "the Phoebes should, therefore, constitute a part of the *diakonoi* of every fully organized congregation."

Moses E. Lard, a well-known evangelist and editor of *Lard's Quarterly*, saw deaconesses as part of the apostolic order. Though he at one time denied a place for deaconesses, he gave strong support by the mid 1870s. "Did Phebe belong to an order of official women in the church?" Lard asked in 1875. "She certainly belonged to an order of women called *servants of the church*, who performed their service by apostolic sanction; and the duties of this order were the same as those usually ascribed to deaconesses." He concluded that "Phebe was a deaconess in the official sense of that word." As a result, he urged, present-day churches should have them too: "whenever the necessities of the churches are such as to demand it, the order of the deaconesses should be re-established. They are often of as much importance to a church as the deacons, if not even more."

Some southern church leaders like David Lipscomb and E. G. Sewell held somewhat different views. While men like Campbell, Pendleton, Milligan, and Lard viewed the eldership and diaconate as offices or official positions in the

E. G. Sewell (1830–1924): one of numerous nineteenth-century church leaders who believed that both men and women could be appointed deacons.

church, Lipscomb and Sewell rejected all "officialism" in the church (see Chapter 14). Elders and deacons, in their view, were not officers but rather simply Christians who possessed certain qualifications and did certain work. One became an elder by doing the work of an elder; one became a deacon by doing the work of a deacon.

In Sewell's view women were not "official" deaconesses, any more than men were "official" deacons. Both men and women occupied exactly the same role—

appointed servants, nothing more. "There is absolutely nothing in the use of the Greek word [*diakoneoo*], nor in a correct translation of it," he argued, "to justify such an *official* idea."

Sewell was troubled to see "a specific class of men in the church called 'deacons,'" for he believed that the term should be applied "to any that serves in any capacity in the church." "Even Phebe was a deacon—a deaconess as men would say now." "Hence any one the church may appoint or request to do any work for them that is in harmony with the word of God," he concluded, "may be called a 'deacon, servant, or minister.'"

Two distinct positions favoring the appointment of deaconesses emerged in the nineteenth-century movement. One position argued for an official order of deaconesses (Campbell, Pendleton, Milligan, and Lard). The other insisted that there was no official order of deacons or deaconesses but that anyone—male or female—could be appointed by the church for a specific work (Lipscomb, Sewell, and others).

Neither position carried the day among Churches of Christ in the late nineteenth century. Lipsomb and Sewell's position was steadily supplanted by "officialism." The "office" of elder and the "office" of deacon solidified rapidly. But the "office" of deaconess—practiced by some in the early movement and advocated by a good many—virtually vanished.

One basic reason was that the churches in the South almost totally accepted the place assigned to women by the dominant culture of Victorian America (see Chapter 17). That place was the domestic sphere. The ideal of "true womanhood," which was becoming dominant by mid-century, underscored woman's submissiveness and domesticity. It placed strong taboos on women in any public leadership roles and drew a tight fence around the home, her God-given sphere.

In the early twentieth-century movement a few male leaders spoke out in favor of deaconesses. One was C. R.

Nichol, an influential Texas preacher. "It should be known in every congregation," he wrote in 1938, "that Sister Phoebe, Sister Priscilla, and Sister Dorcas are deaconesses in the congregation, and that when their assistance is needed they are to be called." He added that "Many congregations are falling short of the work that should be done, because they do not have women appointed to do certain work for the church....As there was a need for the deaconess in the early days of the church, so there is now."

Though a few like Nichol spoke out, few congregations seem to have considered appointing women as deacons, and virtually no congregations actually did so. Women of course continued to do a great deal of the serving in the churches—as they always had. That, after all, was what they took to be Phoebe's place.

Selected Sources

Epigraph: Lard, *Commentary on Paul's Letter to the Romans*, p. 452.

Campbell, Alexander. "The Deacon's Office." *Christian Baptist* 4 (May 1827), 212.

_____. "Order of the Church as Respects Worship." *Millennial Harbinger—Extra* (October 1835), 507-11.

Fanning, Tolbert. "The Church of Christ in History, No. 8." *Religious Historian* (December 1873), 353-61.

Ferguson, Everett; Tom Olbricht; and R. L. Roberts, Jr. "The Journal of the Church of Christ in Kelton, Pennsylvania." *Restoration Quarterly* 13 (1970), 239-42.

Lard, Moses E. *Commentary on Paul's Letter to the Romans*. 1875; Des Moines, IA: Eugene Smith, 1914.

Milligan, Robert. *An Exhortation and Defense of the Scheme of Redemption*. Cincinnati, 1869.

Nichol, C. R. *God's Woman*. Clifton, TX: Nichol, 1938.

Pendleton, W. K. "Deacons—Should the Church Have Them?" *Millennial Harbinger* 41 (1870), 50-54.

_____. "Discipline, No. VII." *Millennial Harbinger*, 3rd Series, 5 (1848), 289-95.

Rothman, Sheila M. *Woman's Proper Place: A History of Changing Ideals and Practices, 1870 to the Present*. New York: Basic Books, 1978.

Sandifer, J. Stephen. *Deacons: Male and Female?* Houston: by the author, 1988. [I am indebted to this work for pointing me to many of the original sources used in this chapter.]

Sewell, E. G. "Diakoneoo." *Gospel Advocate* 34 (June 16, 1892), 377.

_____. "What Is the Duty of Deacons in the Congregations?" *Gospel Advocate* (May 25, 1905), 328.

Chapter 19

Simple Trusting Faith

If one is righteous, he does not need to lay up treasures for the future; for as the need arises the supply will come. This is as certain as any other doctrine of God.

—James A. Harding (1914)

"The child of God that is faithfully honest and industrious in seeking food and raiment and trusts in God's promises and prays earnestly to him for the blessings will find them."

E. G. Sewell had written these words in an August 1902 issue of the *Gospel Advocate,* and to them, James A. Harding of Bowling Green, Kentucky, took considerable exception. It was a fine article for the most part, Harding commented, but "in this quotation we find the one spot where Homer nodded."

Christ does not tell Christians they will receive food, clothing, and shelter *if* they work hard for them; indeed, Harding argued, Christ tells them *not* to seek after such things. "Seek not what ye shall eat, and what ye shall drink.... However, seek ye his kingdom, and these things shall be added to you" (Lk. 12:29, 31).

Sewell retorted that God provided food and raiment

only through "certain channels and laws" and that everyone must comply with these laws in order to receive daily bread. Harding, in reply, underscored his basic point: "God does not want a man in his service to work for and seek food and raiment, for the simple reason that if a man works for and seeks to please him as he should, God will see to it that he gets food, raiment, and everything else he needs."

This exchange with E. G. Sewell highlights one of the central and constant themes in the life of James A. Harding (1848-1914). He called it the "law of special providence." This biblical "law," he said, means that one who gives his all to Christ and his kingdom "is as certain to be supplied with all that he needs as that Christ reigns." No biblical teaching was more sure than this one, he stated, and no biblical teaching gave the believer more joy, confidence, and freedom from worry.

James Harding emerged in the closing decades of the nineteenth century as a leading evangelist, debater, and educator among Churches of Christ. For seventeen years he engaged in full time evangelistic work, going wherever he was called and never setting any fee for his services. "He rose to lofty heights when in the pulpit," H. Leo Boles wrote, "swaying his audience with his fiery earnestness and his childlike faith in the word of God."

Harding also engaged in over fifty debates throughout his career. The most famous was an 1889 debate with the Baptist J. B. Moody in Nashville which was attended nightly by over 2,000 people. Though Harding much preferred evangelism, he was quick, fair, and skilled on the debate platform, and felt that debates accomplished much good for the cause of true Christianity.

Harding spent his later years as a pioneering educator. In 1891 he and David Lipscomb opened the Nashville Bible School, and Harding presided over the school for ten years. In 1900 he moved to Bowling Green, Kentucky, to open Potter

James A. Harding (left) with David Lipscomb: "A man is thoroughly insured, fully provided for all circumstances, if he trusts and obeys God."

Bible College, where he served eleven years as president. During these years he also edited and wrote extensively for a periodical he named *The Way*.

Early in his preaching career, Harding established firm convictions about God's "special providence." While he was still a young preacher a wealthy, dedicated Christian businessman came to him one day and said, "I cannot preach, but I can make money; that is my gift; you can preach, but won't get much money for it." So, he offered, "just let me know when you need any money, and I will be glad to let you have it."

Harding said that some time later he asked to borrow twenty-five dollars. The man gladly wrote out a check and, refusing to take Harding's promissory note, said, "It gives me more pleasure to let you have it, than it does you to receive it." Thereafter, Harding went to him numerous times for money.

But after a while Harding had second thoughts about this arrangement. After pondering Philippians 4:6 and 19, he said, "I began to understand that God desires his children to look to him as their patron, and not to any one else." As a result he decided not to ask his patron for any more money. Temptation beset him at times, he said, but he resisted. "I got along just as well, met every obligation just as promptly, and had the consolation of knowing that I was trusting in God, not in man."

Harding said he was about thirty years old when he reached the basic conviction about God's providence that was to guide the rest of his life and ministry. He concluded that "I need not concern myself in the least about the support of myself and my family, if only I would devote myself wholly, and with due diligence, to the service of God." "I believed I would be supported just as well when working among the poor as when serving the rich," he later wrote, "and that I would be as well cared for where we had no church as where we had large, rich ones."

With this conviction, Harding said that he tried to choose his work by the needs of the kingdom "without taking into consideration my financial interests at all, except to believe that God would supply my every need, if I worked faithfully for him." His only employment contract, he said, was a Matthew 6:33 contract—"Seek first his kingdom and his righteousness, and all these things shall be yours as well." Such a contract guarantees everything one needs, no matter the circumstances, he insisted. It does not depend on whether one pleases people or not, on sickness or on health, or on the size of one's family—but only upon pleasing the Lord. Such a contract makes one free like nothing else, Harding believed, for God is a friend more loving and kind than any earthly father or mother, and his promises of care and blessing are more sure.

The Bible was full of God's promises to take special care of those who trusted him, Harding said, and he frequently recited them in his writings.

- For the eyes of the Lord run to and fro throughout the whole earth, to show his might in behalf of those whose heart is blameless toward him (2 Chron. 16:9).

- And do not seek what you are to eat and what you are to drink, nor be of anxious mind....Instead, seek his kingdom, and these things shall be yours as well (Lk. 12:29, 31).

- Have no anxiety about anything, but in everything by prayer and supplication with thanksgiving let your requests be made known to God....And my God will supply every need of yours according to his riches in glory in Christ Jesus (Phil. 4:6, 19).

- Keep your life free from the love of money, and be content with what you have; for he has said, "I will never fail you nor forsake you" (Heb. 13:5).

For the rest of his life, Harding attempted to take such passages at face value and to live under God's "law of special providence." "For thirty-six years," he wrote in 1910, "I have endeavored to follow the directions of Jesus literally. I have avoided the accumulation of property....I have no house, no land, no stock, no property except that which we daily use, no money laid up for the future." He said that he rarely possessed as much as fifty dollars at one time and, when he did, most often used it for immediate needs.

On another occasion, he said that he had made

preaching tours covering thousands of miles, preaching for churches containing from two to two dozen members, and yet "fared just as well as when I took pay from the school and preached for the large, rich churches." Never, he concluded, had he ever really needed anything that he had not received in due time. Indeed, "God meant just what he said to a cent" and "keeps his word to a dot."

The theme of God's "special providence" was one of the most prominent in Harding's voluminous writings over the years. He returned to it again and again, for he believed that the widespread failure to trust God's promise to care for his people constituted the single "greatest hindrance to the spread of the gospel."

Many Christians do not believe that God takes special care of the temporal needs of the faithful, Harding charged. Many believe, rather, that God made the world according to certain natural laws, and that one who hopes to live well must simply work according to those laws. In this view, "the vilest sinner has as good a prospect for these blessings as the purest saint." Others believe that God has no special temporal blessings for anybody, Harding said, while still others believe that God provided such blessings under the old covenant but not under the new. Many Christians, in other words, "do not believe in special providence, but in the reign of law."

Such disbelief, Harding pointed out time and again, turned Christians' heads away from kingdom business to worldly affairs—to preoccupation with money, food, and raiment. The questions preoccupying most people, even most Christians, were: What shall we eat? Where shall we live? What shall we drive? What if we get sick? How shall we live in our old age? How much will we leave our children?

Absorption in these concerns, Harding believed, was the chief obstacle to doing the Lord's work, and building up the kingdom. Christians spend so much time trying to earn more money and thus secure their lives for the future that they have little money or energy to pour into evangelism. They do not believe God will guide, shelter, cloth, feed, and care for them as he has promised. "Unbelief is the trouble," Harding said.

Indeed, Harding said, Christians habitually violate three basic commands of God:

"Do not lay up for yourselves treasures on earth."

"Do not be anxious about your life, what you shall eat, nor about your body, what you shall put on."

"Be not therefore anxious for the morrow, for the morrow will be anxious for itself."

These promises and commands, Harding stressed, are just as plain and certain as "He that believes and is baptized shall be saved"; to reject one teaching is just as much unbelief as to reject the other. "If we work faithfully for God," he wrote, "the living will come as certainly as remission of sins comes to the man who is baptized into Christ. And much more of the Bible is devoted to teaching the former than to the latter."

Over the years a good many Christians took offense at Harding's doctrine of "special providence." They often accused him of teaching that Christians did not need to work diligently. But he repeatedly denied such a conclusion. Indeed, Christians should work—all honest work, however humble, was appropriate. The Christian should "run that farm, conduct that store, teach that school, spend that money as a slave of Jesus—as one who must give account to his Master for everything."

But—and this was Harding's insistent point—one should not accumulate more than one's daily needs demand. One should not build stockpiles for the future or attempt to lay up a secure inheritance for one's children. One should use the money now—to help the poor, to preach the gospel, to care for the afflicted. God will take care of the future.

But just how will God do that, Harding's many opponents asked? Does God not ordain that people work according to fixed natural laws? Do you expect God to work miracles? Harding answered that, yes, God works through natural laws, but that there are far more such laws than people ever dreamed of, and God can use all of them to care for his people. "There are millions of natural laws that we know nothing about that God knows and uses with perfect ease," he wrote; and furthermore, "he has all the host of angels to do his bidding."

Undergirding Harding's doctrine of "special providence" was his conviction that God held the future firmly in his control. Indeed, like his friend David Lipscomb (Chapter 12), Harding believed that God would one day triumph over all human kingdoms and establish his kingdom fully on the earth. At the chosen time—perhaps about the year 2000—Christ would return, gather his people out of earth's kingdoms, and defeat all the kings of the earth as they rose up against him. Satan then would be cast into the abyss for a thousand years.

"During this time, this thousand years," Harding wrote, "Christ and his saints reign; but the rest of the dead live not again till the thousand years have expired." "This millennial reign will be on the earth," Harding made clear, and it will be a time when Christians will enjoy a "perfect rest from sin."

In view of Christ's coming reign, Christians should "forsake the governments of this world" and devote themselves completely to Christ's kingdom. "We should have nothing to do with appointing or electing officers for the governments of Satan," Harding concluded. "Let us devote all of our energies, powers, and possessions to the kingdom of Christ, which during that last thousand years will fill the whole earth."

For Harding the future was not in doubt: Christ reigned, and his kingdom was sure—and one day soon it would triumph. God's providential care for the believer was built squarely on that triumph, for the one who seeks first the kingdom, Harding declared, "is as certain to be supplied with all that he needs as that Christ reigns."

Simple, trusting faith in God's daily care—that, Harding often said, was the "greatest need of the church."

Selected Sources

Epigraph: James A. Harding, "The Secret of Success, Financially and Otherwise, in Evangelistic Work," *Gospel Herald* 2 (March 5, 1914), 1.

Armstrong, J. N. "The Kingdom of God Destined to Conquer and Own the World." *Gospel Herald* 3 (January 21, 1915), 3, 6.

Harding, James A. "Brother Sewell's Article on 'God's Care.'" *The Way* 2 (December 1900), 148-49.

_____. "The Greatest Hindrance to the Spread of the Gospel." *The Way* 3 (March 6, 1902), 377-79.

_____. "In Whom Shall We Trust?" *The Way* 3 (April 18, 1901), 18-20.

_____. "Jehovah Defeats Wise Counsel." *Gospel Herald* 1 (February 20, 1913), 1, 3.

_____. "The Kingdom of Christ Vs. the Kingdom of Satan." *The Way* 5 (October 15, 1903), 929-31.

_____. "Scraps." *The Way* 4 (April 10, 1902), 10-11.

_____. "Some Notable Cases of Special Providence." *The Way* 4 (July 3, 1902), 106-107.

_____ and L. S. White. *The Harding-White Discussion.* Cincinnati: F. L. Rowe, 1910.

Sears, L. C. *The Eyes of Jehovah: The Life and Faith of James A. Harding.* Nashville: Gospel Advocate, 1970.

Sewell, E. G. "God's Care." *The Way* 2 (December 1900), 147-48.

Chapter 20

How to Deal with Division

I propose never to stand identified with one special wing, branch, or party of the church. My aim is to preach the gospel, do the work of an evangelist, [and] teach God's children how to live.

—T. B. Larimore

In July of 1897 the *Christian Standard* published "An Open Letter to T. B. Larimore" written by one of Larimore's former students. The letter was full of admiration for Larimore and his work, but it contained an urgent request. "You owe it to yourself, your family, your friends, your Saviour and your God," urged Oscar Spiegel of Birmingham, Alabama, "to speak out on some matters now retarding the progress of the cause of Christ." One cannot remain silent, he insisted, "when we see our fellow men, and especially our own family drifting apart."

Spiegel then came to the point. He asked Larimore to declare himself on four key issues that were deeply dividing the restoration movement: the use of instrumental music in worship, the creation of missionary societies beyond the local church, attendance at "cooperative meetings," and salary contracts for preachers.

T. B. Larimore (1843–1929) as a young preacher: "I propose to finish my course without ever, even for one moment, engaging in partisan strife with anybody about anything."

"Thousands of your brethren and sisters," Spiegel concluded, "believe it is your duty to speak out on these questions, and strive to unite, if possible, the people of God."

This closing appeal suggests something of T. B. Larimore's stature in the restoration movement of the late nineteenth century. After his baptism in 1864 and several years of teaching and preaching, Larimore moved to Florence, Alabama, where in 1871 he began Mars Hill Academy. He conducted the school for six months each year, and spent the other six months in evangelistic work.

Throughout the 1870s and 80s Larimore became widely known as an evangelist and by the mid 80s was receiving hundreds of invitations from congregations each year. In 1887, after 17 years, he closed the school to devote himself entirely to evangelism.

That same year he held his first major evangelistic meeting in Nashville; it lasted six weeks and resulted in 126 additions to the church. In 1888 he preached a month in Sherman, Texas, with 50 conversions, and in 1891 for nine weeks at the Campbell St. Church in Louisville, Kentucky, with 108 conversions. An 1895 meeting in Los Angeles, California, lasted three months and saw 125 responses.

He preached for large congregations and small, and traveled the country from South to North and East to West. He averaged over 700 sermons per year and baptized thousands. According to F. D. Srygley, his close friend and biographer, Larimore was the best-known evangelist in the southern part of the movement in the late nineteenth century.

Larimore's prominence arose in a time when the deep tensions in the movement, which long had been present, were erupting in open division in many congregations. Division had begun appearing in the late 1860s and early 70s in northern cities and by the 1880s had spread to conservative strongholds in the West and South. At the congregational level, division often centered around the use of organs in the worship assembly.

The spreading controversies brought much pain and bitterness. As congregations wrangled, outside arbitrators sometimes were brought in and lawsuits sometimes were filed. The movement's journals were filled with intense argument, invective, charge and counter-charge. People faced enormous pressures to take sides and become ardent partisans. Most did.

T. B. Larimore, however, was one who did not. Despite the strong and incessant voices pressuring him to take sides, he simply refused. Year after year, he refused. In many letters and sermons, Larimore made his conviction and practice clear. "My earnest desire," he wrote, "is to keep entirely out of all unpleasant wrangles among Christians....I propose to finish my course without ever, even for one moment, engaging in partisan strife with anybody about anything."

Accordingly, when someone asked him what "wing" of the church he belonged to, the loyal or the digressive, Larimore replied: "I propose never to stand identified with one special wing, branch, or party of the church. My aim is to preach the gospel, do the work of an evangelist, teach God's children how to live, and, as long as I do live, to live as nearly an absolutely perfect life as possible."

Larimore's convictions were tested in 1894. In late 1893 the Houston Street Church in Sherman, where Larimore had held a meeting in 1888, issued an urgent call for him to help them. A pro-organ group had brought an organ into the church building, and many members opposed it. Both sides had threatened to withdraw, and they wanted Larimore to help reunite them.

Larimore agreed. On January 3, 1894, he began an evangelistic meeting with the congregation—and he agreed to preach as long as it seemed good was being accomplished. The meeting continued daily for twenty-two weeks, and produced 254 additions to the congregation.

Nine weeks into the meeting Larimore wrote to a close friend: "You are anxious to know how I am holding up. I am well. Nothing can be better for me than to preach twice every day and three times on Sunday, unless it is to preach three times every day and Sunday too." His correspondent wondered how he managed to find enough preaching material. "Exhaust Bible themes and thoughts and truths at this rate, after a while?" Larimore replied. "Yes, *when swallows drink the ocean dry."*

Throughout the whole marathon meeting, Larimore never mentioned the divisive organ issue. He did as he always did—preached the gospel, baptized, and taught people how to live. He sided with no wing or faction.

In the months following Larimore's departure, the tensions flared again and the congregation split. Eventually the pro-organ group agreed to leave and begin a new congregation. A progressive Disciple journal in Dallas later charged that Larimore was responsible for the division, and a vigorous exchange ensued between the *Gospel Advocate* and the Dallas journal. Larimore, as was his long practice, did not respond to the charges or attempt to defend himself. He was disappointed and hurt, however, that in the years that followed many pro-organ churches in Texas no longer invited him to preach.

In his preaching and writing, Larimore simply never addressed the doctrinal issues dividing the movement. He viewed them as "untaught questions among us." Scripture did not address them, he said; and, though he held his own "opinions or preferences," he did not feel it his duty to preach or write about them.

When Larimore read O. P. Spiegel's "Open Letter" in the *Christian Standard* of July 1897, he responded as he had always responded to the mounting pressure to take sides: he refused. "Never, publicly or privately, have I expressed opinion or preference relative to any of these 'matters'... over which brethren are wrangling and disputing and dividing the church of Christ—NEVER."

Never, he insisted, had he furnished any evidence that he was either for or against the organ or the missionary society. Rather, "I am for Christ," he said; "and I believe I can do more for him, his cause and humanity without meddling with these 'matters'; hence I let them alone, and just simply 'preach the Word,' 'the gospel of Christ,' 'the power of God

Larimore baptizing: "I just simply 'preach the Word,' 'the gospel of Christ,' 'the power of God unto salvation.'"

unto salvation.'"

Larimore then reemphasized his refusal to make these issues matters of fellowship. "While thousands have stood before me, hand in mine, and made 'the good confession,'" he wrote, "I have never questioned one of them about these 'matters.' Shall I now renounce and disfellowship all of these who do not understand these things exactly as I understand them? They may refuse to recognize or fellowship or affiliate with me; but I will never refuse to recognize or fellowship or affiliate with them—NEVER."

Wise and good people stand on both sides, he said, and they often criticize, accuse, and condemn each other. They call each other "antis," "digressives," "mossbacks," and other terms of opprobrium. They easily assume that the good is all on one side and the bad all on the other. But it isn't. "I am as apt to be wrong as my brother," Larimore concluded, for "neither of us is infallible." For this reason, Larimore asserted, "I must love my brethren, and never refuse to fellowship them—ANY OF THEM—simply because we do not always understand all questions exactly alike."

Larimore's response to the "Open Letter" was the strongest and fullest expression of what, for him, remained a life-long stance. Critics railed at him for such a stance. Partisans on one side thought him soft, while partisans on the other side sometimes thought him disloyal.

David Lipscomb, for example, thought Larimore was shirking his duty. "God does not give man the privilege of standing on neither side," he wrote; "he only gives him the privilege of standing on the right or wrong side." "If Brother Larimore does not stand for what is right," Lipscomb concluded, "he stands for what is wrong."

Because the progressive Disciples tended to shut him out, Larimore gradually became identified more and more with the Churches of Christ. But Larimore did not erect the barriers. He continued to write for the *Christian Standard* and to maintain relationships with many people in the other "wing" of the movement. His name remained on the list of preachers in the Disciples Yearbook until 1925, four years before his death.

Among Churches of Christ, Larimore remained an esteemed and beloved preacher. He preached widely and wrote extensively right up to his death in 1929 at age 86. When he died the tributes to his life and ministry virtually filled two whole issues of the *Gospel Advocate*.

Selected Sources

Epigraph: F. D. Srygley, *Smiles and Tears*, p. 260.

Foster, Douglas A. *As Good as the Best: A Sketch of the Life of Theophilus Brown Larimore*. Nashville: Learning Skills, 1984.

_____. "Holding Back the Tide: T. B. Larimore and the Disciples of Christ and Churches of Christ Division." Forrest F. Reed Lecture, Disciples of Christ Historical Society, November 3, 1991. [I am indebted to this paper for many of the references used in this chapter.]

Larimore, T. B. "Preach the Word." *Christian Standard* 33 (January 9, 1897), 44.

_____. "Reply to O. P. Spiegel's Open Letter." *Christian Standard* 33 (July 24, 1897), 965.

Larimore, Mrs. T. B. *Life, Letters and Sermons of T. B. Larimore*. Nashville: Gospel Advocate, 1931.

Letters and Sermons of T. B. Larimore. Edited by F. D. Srygley and Emma Page. 3 vols. Nashville: Gospel Advocate, 1900, 1904, 1910.

Lipscomb, David. "Brother Larimore's Letter." *Gospel Advocate* 39 (August 12, 1897), 500.

Spiegel, O. P. "An Open Letter to T. B. Larimore." *Christian Standard*

33 (July 10, 1897), 891.

Srygley, F. D. *Smiles and Tears, or Larimore and His Boys*. Nashville: Gospel Advocate, 1889.

Chapter 21

What Is the Gospel?

*What this sinful world needs is not 'plans' and
'schemes' but Christ. When Christ crucified is
not preached one should not preach at all....
Let us preach Christ or nothing.*

—K. C. Moser (1952)

In 1932 an Oklahoma preacher named K. C. Moser (1893-
1976) published a small book entitled *The Way of Salvation*.
The book addressed central New Testament themes: the
nature of human sin, the righteousness of God, Christ's
atoning death, justification by faith, and the indwelling of
the Holy Spirit. It did not make a big splash, even though G.
C. Brewer, reviewing it in the *Gospel Advocate*, called it "one
of the best little books that came from any press in 1932."

The book began with a careful and methodical expo-
sition of sin and the need for redemption. But soon it became
clear that something was troubling Moser. Throughout the
book ran a subtle but steady polemic: somebody was miscon-
struing the saving work of Christ and seriously compromising
the gospel.

In the next few years Moser became more pointed and specific. A 1934 article entitled "Can the Gospel Be Obeyed?" critiqued and rejected the traditional formulation of the gospel among Churches of Christ ("facts to be believed, commands to be obeyed, and promises to be received"). Then in a 1937 tract entitled "Are We Preaching the Gospel?" Moser stated flatly that much of the preaching among Churches of Christ could not properly be called gospel preaching.

True gospel preaching, Moser charged, had been eclipsed by what he termed the "plan theory." In this approach Christ's death became simply a somewhat arbitrary means to an end—the end being the giving of a divine plan of salvation. Christ's obedience unto death gave him the authority to set forth a "plan" consisting of four basic stipulations: faith, repentance, confession, and baptism.

Preaching thus focused on the "plan"—on what people must do—not on Christ and his role as sin-bearer. The "plan," in fact, was not intimately connected to Christ's death at all— rather, by his death Christ simply gained the authority to institute the plan. In the preaching of this plan, Moser observed, the cross usually "receives little or no emphasis" for it was simply one step in the giving of the "plan."

The burden of Moser's 1932 book, and most of his writing in the years that followed, was to set forth the gospel over against the dominant "plan theory." He stressed time and again that "Christ brought, not another code, but his precious blood. And by it sinners are redeemed. Our iniquities were laid upon him, and 'with his stripes we were healed.'" "Christ crucified for sinners," Moser insisted, "is the divine 'plan' of salvation."

Moser was not alone in his pointed concerns. Another outspoken preacher who shared many of Moser's concerns was G. C. Brewer (1883-1956). Though Brewer was a debater and a controversialist by nature and Moser was not, the two men were good friends. On preaching trips they sometimes stayed in each other's homes, and over the years maintained a high regard for one another.

In his review of Moser's book, Brewer wrote that many Christians have made the gospel "a system of divine laws for human beings to obey and thus save themselves sans grace, sans mercy, sans everything spiritual and divine— except that the 'plan' was in mercy given."

In the years that followed, Brewer, like Moser, continued to critique this "plan" theory. "To trust a plan is to expect to save yourself by your own works," he wrote in 1945. "It is to build according to a blueprint; and if you meet the specifications your building will be approved by the great Inspector! Otherwise you fail to measure up and you are lost!"

"That is all wrong, brethren!" Brewer exclaimed. "We have a Savior who saves us. We throw ourselves upon his mercy, put our case in his hands, and submit gladly and humbly to his will. That is our hope and our only hope."

Moser and Brewer fully agreed on a basic point: "The whole story of human redemption is comprehended in two words: 'grace' and 'faith.' It is grace on God's part and faith on man's part."

Both men insisted that, although human obedience was necessary for salvation, it was "not a matter of law." "Our salvation does not depend upon our perfect adherence to the requirements of law," Brewer wrote. "By making our salvation dependent upon our own perfection, we make void the grace of God. And to make our perfection a matter of legal requirements fully met would make Christ's death useless." He added that "We should be careful not to affirm the abrogation of one law and then substitute another law and make salvation dependent upon the same principal."

Moser's fullest and most explicit critique of the "plan theory" came in a 1952 pamphlet entitled *Christ Versus a "Plan."* Here he gave four fundamental reasons why he

K. C. Moser (left) with G.C. Brewer in 1929: both men spoke out against the "plan" theory and called for a grace-centered message.

rejected such an approach.

(1) *It removes Christ and the cross from first place and puts central emphasis on the "plan."* "Times almost without number," Moser reported, "I have heard sermons on the conditions of salvation without a single reference to the cross. I have heard preaching in meetings that lasted for three weeks in which the cross of Christ received only a passing reference. But in every sermon a 'plan' was preached and sinners urged to do their 'duty.' The 'plan' was considered the gospel unto salvation."

Moser found it strange and disturbing that many preachers could spend so little time on the meaning of Jesus' death and yet spend so much on obeying the "plan." How, he wondered, could they virtually omit "the very thing that makes Jesus the Savior and preach the conditions apart from him."

Moser's most fundamental complaint was that people were giving emphasis to a "plan of salvation" that belongs to Christ himself. They were "magnifying the conditions of salvation apart from Christ crucified." Christ did not direct people to a "plan," Moser insisted, but to himself—the full and final sacrifice for sin. None of the apostles preached a "plan," but rather Christ crucified. "Peter's subject on Pentecost was not repentance or baptism," he said, "but Christ. And it was after preaching Christ as the Messiah that he commanded anyone to do anything."

(2) *The "plan theory" views the conditions of salvation as arbitrarily given by God.* People who preached the "plan," according to Moser, tended to say that God could have used some other plan, some other conditions of salvation, but he chose faith, repentance, confession, and baptism. One must not expect to know why, one must simply obey.

When Moser read such a statement from a well-known preacher, he was aghast. When a doctor diagnoses an illness and prescribes a remedy, Moser asked, does the patient not know why he must take the medicine? So with the so-called "conditions of salvation." Sin is the illness, and it necessitates repentance or turning away from sin. Jesus' blood supplies the remedy, and it necessitates faith or trust in him. "It is as naturally required of sinners to have faith in Jesus as it is required of the hungry person to eat food." And baptism, because it embodies or expresses repentance and trust, is a natural response to the blood of Christ.

(3) *The "plan theory" makes the "plan" the means of salvation, not Christ crucified.* "If we are saved by a 'plan,'" Moser

asked, "does this not make the 'plan' our savior? Is there life in a 'plan'? Is a 'plan' redemptive? Jesus thought that he died to save sinners. If he died to give us a 'plan' by which to be saved, then it is not his death by which we are saved, but the 'plan' given by reason of his death."

For Moser the crux of the matter was this: "When the saving power is separated from the personal Christ and located in something accomplished by Jesus after his death, he no longer is the Savior. He is only the giver of that which saves." The truth of the matter, Moser said, is that "Jesus himself, God's Son, crucified for our sins is the only 'plan' of salvation possible, and he is never so designated [in the New Testament]!"

(4) *The "plan theory" misconceives the meaning of saving faith and obedience to Christ.* If faith as trust in Christ is distorted, Moser said, so is obedience to him: "When the conditions of salvation are regarded as a 'plan,' the obedience required of the sinner is considered merely the response to the authority of Christ." But obedience to Christ does not simply spring from the fact that Christ is now king and has the right to command. Rather, obedience flows directly out of one's trust in Christ as the sin-offering. Indeed, such trust, Moser insisted, is obedience.

He made it clear that one certainly should not preach Christ "apart from the conditions of salvation." But, he added, "I do with all my heart condemn preaching the conditions of salvation apart from the cross. I have heard it done a thousand times!" In doing this one failed to preach Christ as Savior—and there could be "no error greater" in preaching than this.

Moser concluded his pamphlet with these words: "What this sinful world needs is not 'plans' and 'schemes' but Christ. When Christ crucified is not preached one should not preach at all....Let us preach Christ or nothing."

After reading *Christ Versus a "Plan,"* a young preacher

and Christian college professor wrote to Moser in August 1953. He agreed wholeheartedly with Moser's rejection of the "plan theory," and thanked him profusely for his insights into the gospel.

But the young preacher was also troubled. "You know as well as I," he wrote, "that the vast majority, yea all but a pitiful few, take the 'plan' approach to the preaching of the 'gospel,' perhaps unwittingly." As a result, he continued, the churches are filled with two types of people: "those who have been justified by a 'plan'" and are "perfectly confident that 'we' have 'the truth'"; and "those who *want* Christ" but are not being fed the robust food of the gospel.

He wondered if "our brethren are hopelessly lost in legalism?" And he confessed that he had found preaching somewhat "like trying to turn the ocean red by pouring in a gallon of paint."

Over the years of his ministry Moser received numerous letters like this one. But his writing and teaching also brought sharp—and sometimes devastating—opposition. According to one of his daughters, the many attacks he received in the 1930s severely affected his health. Beginning about 1932 he began suffering from what was later diagnosed as ulcerative colitis. By 1935 it had grown so severe that his wife felt he was going to die.

His daughter later wrote of these years: "I was the baby sister that everyone protected, and though I was painfully aware that he was a sick man most of my growing up years, I didn't really know why until I was grown and understood the deep, personal wounds that my father had received."

About 1935 Moser sought help at the famous Mayo Clinic, but was told that only a major change in his life would help. He changed. He quit full-time preaching and began spending most of his time on his farm near Lubbock, Texas. And it so happened that his good friend G. C. Brewer was preaching in Lubbock during those years, and that friend-ship buoyed his spirits.

By 1940 Moser had recovered sufficiently to return to full-time preaching, and served effectively for a number of years. In semi-retirement throughout the 1950s and 60s, he preached by appointment, taught Bible at Lubbock Christian College, and continued his writing.

In 1955 he wrote and published a hymn entitled "Glory, Lord, to Thee." It well captures the central theme of all his writing and preaching.

> Lord, before Thy cross I bow,
> Human merit disavow;
> Trustingly I look to Thee for cleansing pow'r.
> Glory, glory, Lord, to Thee,
> For redemption full and free;
> Glory, honor be to Thee for evermore.

As the years passed the insistent call to focus on Christ rather than a "plan" gradually found a more receptive audi-ence. As Moser, G. C. Brewer, and a few others pressed the matter, a growing number of church members began rethinking the traditional formulation of the gospel. The efforts of Moser, Brewer, and these others stand directly behind some of the theological shifts occurring among contemporary Churches of Christ.

Selected Sources

Epigraph: Moser, *Christ Versus a "Plan,"* p. 17.

Brewer, G. C. "Christ Today: Our Mediator and High Priest." In *Abilene Christian College Bible Lectures*, 1938. Austin, Tex.: Firm Foundation, 1938.

_____. "Confession and the Plan of Salvation." *Gospel Advocate* 87 (April 26, 1945), 233.

_____. "Grace and Salvation." *Abilene Christian College Bible Lectures, 1952.* Austin, Tex.: Firm Foundation, 1952.

_____. "Read This Book." *Gospel Advocate* 75 (May 11, 1933), 434.

Moser, K. C. *Are We Preaching the Gospel?* 1937.

_____. "Can the Gospel Be Obeyed?" *Firm Foundation* 51 (February 6, 1934), 2.

_____. *Christ Versus a "Plan."* Searcy, Ark.: Harding College Bookstore, 1952.

_____. "The Meaning of Obedience to Christ." Unpublished manuscript.

_____. "Studies in Romans." Unpublished Notebook.

_____. *The Way of Salvation.* Nashville: Gospel Advocate, 1932.

*I am indebted to Ardis Moser, K. C. Moser's widow, and to Fran Winkles, one of his daughters, for some of the information in this chapter. A few months before her death in August 1990, Mrs. Moser invited me to her home and spent an evening discussing her husband's life and work. Mrs. Winkles also shared her memories with me and made available unpublished papers and letters.

Chapter 22

Distant Voices and Present Challenges

That which we remember is, more often than not, that which we would like to have been; or that which we hope to be. Thus our memory and our identity are ever at odds; our history ever a tale told by inattentive idealists.

—Ralph Ellison (1964)

In the introduction to this book we examined the way we remember our pasts as individuals. Out of the constant rush of experiences we selectively fashion a story. We highlight some experiences, forget others, simplify complex events, and piece together fragments. That story becomes our past, and that past powerfully shapes our present lives.

The way we "remember" our Christian tradition or heritage, I suggested, works somewhat like the way we remember our own personal pasts. The kind of past we remember strongly shapes how we think of ourselves as a church. It limits and focuses the goals we set, the kinds of challenges we will accept, and the dreams we are willing to dream. In a word, the kind of past we remember plays a large part in determining what we can and cannot become.

Religious traditions and institutions, like our own lives, are rich and complex things. Like us, they also possess selective memories with which they invariably develop what we might call an "official" story of their past. This "official" story serves the fundamental purpose of affirming and upholding the tradition. In other words, it tells the story in a way that helps maintain traditional boundaries and that sanctions the generally accepted theological tenets.

But this "official" history typically does not tell the whole story, for Christian traditions also leave behind what we might call a "hidden history." The "hidden history" is the part of the story that gets pushed aside, relegated to the margins, and largely forgotten.

This happens in part because traditions are fundamentally conservative and conformist. They prize stability and resist change. Such a tendency has its large benefits as well as its significant problems. As traditions grow, they seek to contain dissent, to close questions once left open, and to narrow the range of allowable diversity. Traditionalists tend, by reflex, to offer answers already at hand and to discourage the reopening of questions long thought settled.

In the interest of stability and control, a tradition tends to turn away from the quest, with its potential challenges and surprises, and to favor settlement, with its secure boundaries. As that happens, the story of its past tends to get cleaned up, the rough edges smoothed, the strident cords harmonized. Respected leaders tend to become larger than life. Aberrant views held by those leaders tend to get tucked away out of sight. And dissenters often get silenced or painted in somewhat darker colors.

In this way a "hidden history" gets left behind. It consists of the forgotten stories of well-known leaders who held aberrant views, of seekers who were not ready to settle down, of ordinary people who read their own Bibles and thought their own thoughts, and of dissenters who were not powerful enough to gain a dominant place in the tradition.

Churches of Christ have their own "official" history and also a "hidden history," as this book has shown. The contours of the "official" story were set by J. F. Rowe's, *A History of Reformatory Movements Resulting in a Restoration of the Apostolic Church* (1884), then taken up and shaped further by twentieth-century preachers and historians. One finds simplified versions of the story in J. W. Shepherd's *The Church, the Falling Away, and the Restoration* (1929), N. B. Hardeman's series of *Tabernacle Sermons*, and in many tracts, articles, historical charts, and biographical sketches.

How does part of the story get hidden? Does it happen by some conspiracy or some intent to distort the past? No, not usually. Simply put, it gets hidden much the same way that many of our own personal experiences get hidden: we forget them, screen them out, and find some of them irrelevant or disturbing to our present lives.

We must understand something about the past: it is not simply an inert and lifeless body of events and facts. The history of a religious movement—as of an individual life—is not simply the reciting of the facts, of telling what happened next. The way one marshals the facts and shapes the story is guided by the questions one asks, the loyalties one maintains, and the particular challenges at hand.

Barton Stone provides an illuminating case study of how parts of the story got hidden. As we saw in several early chapters, Stone and Campbell, though sharing a central concern for restoring primitive Christianity, differed profoundly in their theological outlooks. They differed sharply regarding the dynamics of conversion, the Spirit's work, and the Trinity. They differed on the nature of Christ's atoning death, fellowship with the unimmersed, and the Christian's relationship to government. And they differed over the nature and demands of discipleship, the possibility of present-day miracles, the earthly reign of Christ, and other doctrinal matters.

But a survey of twentieth-century accounts of Stone among Churches of Christ reveals a quite different picture. One writer noted in 1928 that Stone and Campbell, in their first meeting, discovered "almost perfect agreement between them[selves]." In 1939 another historian wrote that the two men discussed certain issues for a time but soon realized that they held "practically the same" views. In 1945 another wrote that Stone's movement could unite with Campbell's because the two groups were "so nearly in perfect agreement."

More recent accounts list some differences between the two (the name "Christian," frequency of the Lord's Supper, the emphasis on immersion, evangelistic methods, and the contrast between spirit and reason), but they emphasize that the "similarities far outweighed the differences" and note the "ease" with which the union occurred.

In short, the "official" story of Barton Stone among twentieth-century Churches of Christ goes something like this: Stone pioneered the rejection of creeds and the call to unite on the Bible alone; he met up with Campbell and both were struck by the similarity of their views; their two groups readily ironed out a few minor differences and united in 1832, forming the great platform of truth on which the Churches of Christ have stood ever since.

In this twentieth-century story, however, much remains hidden. For one thing, Stone's own extensive writings were overshadowed by those of Campbell and his heirs; thus these writings simply have not been known in later generations. For another, Stone's actual views, had they been known, would not have allowed him to remain an admired and heroic figure in the turn-of-the-century tradition. For he held a wider view of Christian fellowship, a stricter view of Christian discipleship, a larger view of the Holy Spirit's work, and a premillennial view of Christ's return.

Stone's name was too admired and heroic, however, for him to be branded a heretic and cast out. Therefore a simpler story was told, one reflecting what Churches of Christ had become by the early twentieth century. In this way key parts of Stone's story entered the "hidden history."

For a tradition to remain strong and dynamic in the face of changed circumstances and new challenges it needs dialogue between its "official" history and its "hidden history." To discover this "hidden history" is to hear voices that we have not heard—or not been able to hear—for a long time. It is to hear minor chords usually drowned out by the major ones. It is to find, to our surprise, that the theological conversation out of which the twentieth-century Churches of Christ grew was richer, livelier, and more diverse than we knew.

Barton Stone, Nancy Cram, Walter Scott, Alexander Campbell, Robert Richardson, David Lipscomb, B. A. Hinsdale, Silena Holman, T. B. Larimore, James A. Harding, G. C. Brewer, K. C. Moser—these distant voices invite us to pull up a chair and join the lively conversations out of which the tradition took shape.

To listen in is to find new and unexpected resources for today, to catch bright glints of time-tarnished ideals. It does not necessarily mean, of course, accepting all of their views. That would be neither possible nor desirable. And it certainly does not mean creating new larger-than-life heroes as substitutes for older, tarnished ones. Rather, it is to discover a richer, more dynamic past—and to sense again the lure and excitement of the continuing quest for faithfulness.

When that happens, we expand our "memories" and open the door to a richer, more dynamic future, a future ripe with new possibilities and larger dreams.

Selected Sources

Boles, H. Leo. "Barton W. Stone." *Gospel Advocate* (July 12, 1928), 654-55.

Borden, E. M. *Church History, Showing the Origin of the Church of Christ, and Its History from the Days of the Apostles to Our Time.* Austin, TX: Firm Foundation, 1939.

Brumback, Robert W. *History of the Church through the Ages: From the Apostolic Age, through the Apostasies, the Dark Ages, the Reformation, and the Restoration.* St. Louis: Mission Messenger, 1957.

Hailey, Homer. *Attitudes and Consequences in the Restoration Movement.* Rosemead, CA: Old Paths Book Club, 1945.

Humble, Bill J. *The Story of the Restoration.* Austin, TX: Firm Foundation, 1969.

Mattox, F. W. *The Eternal Kingdom: A History of the Church of Christ.* Rev. ed. Delight, AR: Gospel Light, 1961.

GROUP DISCUSSION GUIDE

Chapter 1: Discovering a Forgotten Past

1. Share some of the memories from your first ten years of life that stand out most vividly to you. Can you tell why those memories remain vivid?

2. Describe something you have learned as an adult about your family's past that has made you see your family differently.

3. Someone asks you, "Tell me the story of your church—where did it come from, what does its stand for?" If you could give only a two minute answer, what would you say?

4. Analyze your answer to the previous question. What are the sources of your story? How did you learn to tell it that way? Has your way of telling the story changed over the years? If so, why?

5. The author suggests that the "way we 'remember' our Christian past or tradition parallels somewhat the way we remember our own personal pasts." Explore some of these parallels.

6. Define what the author means when he speaks of "distant voices."

7. Why might it be helpful to listen to some of the "distant voices" in a time of change and rethinking?

Chapter 2: Communion Festivals in Kentucky

1. Compare the Scotch-Irish Presbyterian communion service of the seventeenth and eighteenth century with the typical communion service today. Which do you think best captures the earliest Christian practice? Why?

2. Why did revivalistic practices in the eighteenth and nineteenth century prove so divisive among believers? Do you see any similar tensions present today?

3. If you were able, through time travel, to join the throngs at Cane Ridge in early August 1801, how would you have reacted? What would you have said in a letter to your friends back home?

4. Barton Stone was a lifelong supporter of revivals, Alexander Campbell a lifelong foe of them. Why? What theological and personal differences lay behind these opposing assessments?

5. Discuss the five central themes that lay at the heart of Stone's movement. Would these themes describe the central focus of Churches of Christ today? Why or why not?

Chapter 3: *The Only Hope for Unity*

1. Why did the idea of rejecting religious traditions and restoring primitive Christianity became so widespread in the period of early American nationhood? What cultural factors were at work? [For a discussion of five reasons for the popularity of the restoration ideal in this period, see Allen and Hughes, *Discovering Our Roots: The Ancestry of Churches of Christ* (ACU Press, 1988), pp. 90-94.]

2. Why did the revolt against tradition and traditional authorities inevitably result in religious fragmentation? How has that revolt continued to effect Churches of Christ?

3. Why did Barton Stone avoid religious debates? Do you think he was right or wrong?

4. Why did Stone reject the approach he called "Head Union"? How did he think opinions could function like a creed?

5. Why did Stone think that unity would result only through the Spirit's work and not through doctrinal agreement?

6. How have Churches of Christ conceived the basis for Christian unity? What has this meant in practice?

Chapter 4: *Your Daughters Shall Prophesy*

1. What were some of the defining features of Elias Smith's "Christian" movement in New England?

2. What was it about Smith's movement that allowed a place for "female preachers"?

3. What were some of the criticisms leveled against Elias Smith and his movement?

4. How did the conversion experience empower women to step over the boundaries of social convention?

5. How did women like Nancy Towle justify their calls to preach?

6. Describe Nancy Mulkey's work as an "exhorter."

7. How do women use their teaching and exhorting gifts today?

Chapter 5: The Comfort of the Gospel

1. Describe the pattern of conversion in early nineteenth-century revivalism.

2. Why did Alexander Campbell spend so much effort opposing "spiritual influences"?

3. What pitfall might there be in such ardent opposition to "spiritual influences"?

4. According to Campbell, what was the proper order of the conversion process?

5. How did the doctrine of "baptism for remission" bring comfort and assurance to insecure believers? How did this effect Campbell's view of the essentiality of baptism? (see Chapter 8)

6. Has Campbell's view of baptism come down to the present day pretty well intact? How do Churches of Christ address experiential aspects of conversion?

Chapter 6: The True Measure of Fellowship

1. What was the basis for unity between Stone's "Christians" and Campbell's "Disciples" in 1832?

2. Though unity has been one of the central messages of the restoration movement in America, the 1832 union is the only case of actual unity in the movement's history. Why is it so difficult for two religious groups to unite?

3. What doctrinal differences remained when the two groups united in 1832? Evaluate the extent and significance of these differences?

4. Why did Barton Stone consider himself in fellowship with unimmersed believers? Why did Alexander Campbell oppose such fellowship?

5. For what three reasons did Stone not make immersion a test of Christian fellowship?

6. How could Campbell exclude unimmersed believers from

formal fellowship yet not necessarily from salvation?

7. Whose viewpoint has been predominant among Churches of Christ?

Chapter 7: How God Works

1. Summarize the basic difference between Stone and Campbell over how God works in the world. How did this difference shape their views of prayer?

2. Contrast Stone's and Campbell's views of human progress. How could they see the same phenomena and draw such different conclusions?

3. How might one's view of human nature and sinfulness affect one's view of human progress?

4. Contrast Stone's and Campbell's views of conversion. What role did the Holy Spirit play?

5. How do views of conversion tend to correlate with views of how God works on the large stage of human history?

6. Contrast Stone's and Campbell's views of Christian discipleship in the world.

7. Toward which of these two viewpoints would the present-day secular culture gravitate? Why?

8. Toward which of these two viewpoints do present-day Churches of Christ gravitate? Why?

Chapter 8: Who Is a Christian?

1. Why do you think Campbell said, "I cannot make any one duty the standard of Christian state or character, not even immersion"?

2. How did Campbell understand the relationship between immersion and remission of sins? What subtle distinction did he make?

3. Why did Campbell's emphasis on baptism shift somewhat in the mid 1830s?

4. What did he mean by saying that baptism was essential to a believer's "sanctification and comfort"? (For more on this point, refer back to chapter five.)

5. Discuss Campbell's distinction between "inward and outward Christians." Why would he make such a distinction?

6. Are these distinctions made today?

Chapter 9: Room for the Spirit

1. Describe Robert Richardson's relationship to Alexander Campbell.

2. What problem did Richardson see with the controversial spirit in the restoration movement of his day?

3. What was the "dirt philosophy"? Why did Richardson oppose it?

4. What two extremes regarding the Holy Spirit did Richardson oppose? Why?

5. In recent years have Churches of Christ tended toward one of these extremes? If so, how?

6. Summarize Richardson's view of the Holy Spirit's indwelling. What happened to Christian faith without the Spirit? [See also Chapter 11, for Richardson's view of the essence of true religion.]

7. Compare Richardson's view of the Spirit to the revivalism of Barton Stone (see Chapters 2 and 7).

Chapter 10: *The Bond of Peace*

1. What was the inherent problem in the slogan, "In faith unity; in opinions liberty," as seen in the subsequent history of the movement?

2. According to Robert Richardson, what three basic principles did the movement rest upon?

3. Why, in Richardson's view, was it not sufficient to say, "The

Bible alone is our only creed"? Evaluate his distinction between the Bible and the gospel?

4. Richardson thought that people could possess the same faith yet differ greatly in their doctrinal understanding. How was this possible?

5. What did Richardson see as the fundamental cause of division among believers? What do you think is the fundamental cause?

6. Read John 17 and discuss Richardson's distinction between unity and union?

7. Contrast Richardson and Fanning in their understanding of unity and diversity. How do these issues effect the church today?

Chapter 11: Holy Mysteries

1. In Robert Richardson's view, what was the heart of "true religion"? What do you think it is?

2. What were some of the factors that Richardson thought had retarded the spirituality of the movement? [see also Chapter 10]

3. In addition to *Communings in the Sanctuary*, what are some of the other significant devotional books produced by this restoration movement?

4. Why, according to Richardson, was standing before the great mysteries an aid to the spiritual life? Why was this particularly true for the mystery of the atonement?

5. How did Richardson view the relationship between faith and reason. Compare his view to the way Churches of Christ usually have viewed the role of reason in faith.

6. What do you think it means to be united with Christ? [see 1 Cor. 6:15-20; Rom. 6:5-11] React to Richardson's view.

Chapter 12: The Peaceable Kingdom

1. Compare David Lipscomb's view of the kingdom of God with Barton Stone's view (see Chapter 7).

2. What was Lipscomb's view of the origin and status of human governments?

3. According to Lipscomb, what will God's restored kingdom be like? Where will it be established?

4. Explain the relationship between Lipscomb's view of God's kingdom and his understanding of discipleship.

5. What was the theological basis for Lipscomb's pacifism? What is your impression of the status of pacifism among Churches of Christ today?

6. Why was Lipscomb's position so offensive to some leaders of Churches of Christ in the early to mid-twentieth century?

Chapter 13: God's Chosen Vessels

1. Some thought Lipscomb was too judgmental of those who fled the city during the epidemic. What do you think?

2. One of Lipscomb's most basic beliefs was that "the church is the especial legacy of God to the poor of the earth." Evaluate this statement in light of scripture (eg. Deut. 10:17-18; Amos 5:10-15, 6:1-7; Ps. 146; Lk. 4:18-19, 6:20-25, 14:12-14; 1 Cor. 1:26-29; James 2:1-7).

3. Why did Lipscomb think that the common people were "best fitted to maintain and spread" the Christian faith? Do you agree or disagree?

4. Why did he think that wealth usually corrupted the church? How did it effect the church's outreach to the poor?

5. In Lipscomb's view, how can preachers keep their hearts and lives focused on preaching the gospel to the poor?

6. Assess the relevance of Lipscomb's views to churches today.

Chapter 14: *Faithful Shepherds*

1. What effect did the "incorporation" of America have on American churches?

2. Why did David Lipscomb believe that elders possessed no "official" authority?

3. If elders possessed no "official" authority, what kind of authority did they have, according to Lipscomb?

4. In Lipscomb's view, how did one become an elder? How should congregations select them?

5. What were some of the problems with "officialism," as Lipscomb saw it?

6. Contrast Lipscomb's view of elders and deacons with contemporary views.

Chapter 15: *The Trouble with Stained Glass*

1. What were some of the social and cultural factors behind the controversy over the Central Christian Church building?

2. What was the problem with wealth and luxury in the church, according to Benjamin Franklin and Isaac Errett?

3. Why did Isaac Errett change his attitude toward expensive church buildings? On what grounds did he defend the

Central building?

4. Summarize Franklin and J. F. Rowe's criticism of the Central building. How did they see its impact on ministry to the poor?

5. What do church buildings reveal about the values and character of the people who worship in them?

6. How has the church where you worship dealt with this issue?

Chapter 16: The Blessing of Tradition

1. Describe the attitude toward the past and its traditions in the early American nation.

2. Why was there widespread revolt in early America against the established Christian traditions?

3. Describe Alexander Campbell's attitude toward tradition. Do you think he was able to make a clean break with the Christian past, as he claimed?

4. What value did Burke Hinsdale see in the Christian tradition? What pitfalls did it present?

5. Nicholas Wolterstorff wrote: "Modernity began with an assault on tradition; 'Let us start over,' said Descartes and Locke. Slowly and with great reluctance we in the modern

world have come to realize that there can be no starting over, no escape from heritage." React and discuss.

6. List and discuss some of the benefits of tradition for your life and faith.

Chapter 17: The New Woman

1. What were Silena Holman's basic disagreements with David Lipscomb regarding woman's role? What basic views did they share?

2. Lipscomb and many of his colleagues distinguished between public and private realms in their view of woman's role. Holman rejected such a distinction. Is such a distinction legitimate or not?

3. What arguments did Lipscomb use to make the case for woman's strictly domestic role? How would such arguments be received in the church today?

4. Describe the ideal of "true womanhood" as it emerged in the early nineteenth century. What cultural factors shaped it?

5. Contrast the "true woman" with the "new woman."

6. What is the dominant model of womanhood among Churches of Christ today? Assess the role that tradition and culture have played in shaping that model.

7.   What light might the Holman/Lipscomb exchanges shed on present discussions of woman's role?

Chapter 18: Phoebe's Place

1.   Who were some of the nineteenth-century leaders of the restoration movement who favored the appointment of deaconesses?

2.   What two main positions favoring deaconesses emerged in the nineteenth-century church?

3.   Discuss Lipscomb and Sewell's rejection of "officialism" as it related to the appointment and work of deacons.

4.   What position became dominant among Churches of Christ by the twentieth century? Why?

Chapter 19: Simple Trusting Faith

1.   What was the basic disagreement between E. G. Sewell and James Harding regarding God's care for Christians?

2.   Summarize Harding's understanding of the "law of special providence." How did it shape the way he lived?

3.   What are key scriptures that Harding believed taught this doctrine? Do you agree with his interpretation?

4. According to Harding, why was the failure to believe in God's temporal care of Christians the "greatest hindrance to the spread of the gospel"?

5. How did Harding understand the difference between laying up treasure on earth and laying up treasure in heaven?

6. How was Harding's doctrine of "special providence" related to his conviction about the coming triumph of God's kingdom?

7. Some of Harding's opponents accused him of having "too much faith." What do you think?

Chapter 20: *How to Deal with Division*

1. Describe T. B. Larimore's work as an evangelist.

2. What issues were dividing the restoration movement in the closing decades of the nineteen century?

3. Why did Larimore refuse to take sides in the growing division?

4. In his twenty-two week meeting with the Sherman church Larimore never addressed the issue of instrumental music. Do you think he made a serious mistake?

5. What did Larimore mean by "untaught questions"? What do you consider some "untaught questions" that should not

divide believers today?

6. Evaluate Larimore's way of dealing with division among believers.

Chapter 21: What Is the Gospel?

1. Why did K. C. Moser, in the 1930s, believe that much of the preaching among Churches of Christ could not properly be called gospel preaching?

2. Summarize G. C. Brewer's critique of the "plan" theory of the gospel.

3. What two words, according to Moser and Brewer, capsule the whole story of redemption?

4. Why, in Moser and Brewer's view, was salvation "not a matter of law"? Do you agree or disagree?

5. What were Moser's objection to the "plan" theory? What was his most basic objection to this approach?

6. What was Moser's understanding of the relationship between the gospel and the "conditions of salvation"?

7. If you were to write a tract for our times entitled, "Are We Preaching the Gospel?" what are some of the main points you would make?

Chapter 22: Distant Voices and Present Challenges

1. Explore the distinction between "official history" and "hidden history"? How might this apply to family histories? Think of examples and share them.

2. Why do Christian traditions tend to leave behind a hidden history? What factors govern the process of remembering and telling the story?

3. How has Barton Stone been remembered among Churches of Christ? What aspects of his outlook were forgotten?

4. If Stone were alive today, how do you think he would be received among Churches of Christ?

5. What has surprised you most in listening to some of these distant voices? What have you found most helpful?

6. In light of this material, discuss the issue of unity and diversity in the Christian community. How much diversity is allowable? How much uniformity is demanded? What is the source of unity?

Index